W9-AJT-752

ONE NATION UNDER GOD

An Anthology for Americans

Edited by

Robert Gordon Smith

Throughout this wide-ranging anthology —from solemn statements of national purpose to anecdotes and epigrams, from a prayer by George Washington to the Inaugural Address of John F. Kennedy in 1961—a basic unity of outlook attests the permanence of American values. There is a pervading belief in the right of all citizens to equal protection under the law, to equal economic, social, and political opportunities, to freedom of speech and worship. The citizen's duty to participate in community affairs and to sacrifice his private welfare when the general welfare demands it; his desire to help others less fortunate than himself; his faith in the code of Patrick Henry's "just God, who presides over the destinies of nations"— these ideals, too, are recorded in many ways.

This anthology richly represents 185 years of American life and thought. It contains magazine and newspaper articles, historic speeches, letters, and documents; sermons, hymns, prayers, and selections from the Bible of special mean-

(continued on back flap)

One Nation Under God

One Nation Under God

AN ANTHOLOGY FOR AMERICANS

edited by
Robert Gordon Smith

☆

FUNK & WAGNALLS
A Division of READER'S DIGEST BOOKS, INC.
NEW YORK

2

TO

The United States of America

AND ALL WHO SHARE
THE AMERICAN DREAM
OF
FREEDOM AND DIGNITY UNDER GOD
FOR ALL MEN—EVERYWHERE

Foreword

This book speaks for itself. Nothing I say by way of introduction can add to the luster of the American Dream or lend brighter meaning to the words and deeds of all who have made our country great.

We know full well we have a long way yet to go. Our sins are many. Our faults are plain for all to see. Our weaknesses are not hidden from the searching light of truth. But we will triumph over them. We will grow greater in goodness and grace. We will go forward and upward as long as we maintain our liberty, as long as we preserve for all men the right to work, to own property, to speak out and stand up for those things in which they sincerely believe.

And above all, may we never forget that

> *Our help is in the name of the Lord,*
> *who made heaven and earth.   Ps. 124:8.*

> *They that trust in the Lord shall be as*
> *Mount Zion, which cannot be removed, but*
> *abideth forever.   Ps. 125:1.*

God bless our United States, and help us to be true to our best selves, to America, and to Thee.

ROBERT GORDON SMITH

Acknowledgments and Copyright Notices

"Arlington: Where Sleep the Brave" by Donald Culross Peattie, reprinted by permission of World Publishing Company and *The Reader's Digest* from *Parade With Banners* by Donald Culross Peattie. Copyright 1952 by The Reader's Digest Association.

"The Unknown Soldier" by Virginia Eaton, reprinted by permission of the author.

"Inaugural" by Alva Romanes, reprinted by permission of *Weekly Unity.*

"The President Prays" by Ruth Gibbs Zwall, reprinted from *Home,* April, 1956, by permission of the author and the American Baptist Publication Society.

Presidential Inaugural Address by John F. Kennedy, reprinted by permission of the author.

Contents

136 chapters

One Nation Under God

THE PEOPLE'S PRAYER

☆

by *Amos R. Wells* (*1862-1933*)

☆

God bless our dear United States,
Preserve the land from evil fates,
Lift high her banner fair and free,
And guard her bounds from sea to sea.

From foe without and foe within,
From open shame and hidden sin,
From boastful pride and greedy store,
God keep our nation evermore.

Forever may her friendly hands
Receive the poor of other lands
In kindliness of sisterhood,
And fill their arms with ample good.

Assailed by battle hosts of wrong,
God help our country to be strong.
Assailed by falsehood's crafty crew,
God help our country to be true.

God hold the nation's aim sincere,
God save her heart from coward fear.
God prosper her in true success,
And crown her head with worthiness.

God bless our dear United States,
Preserve the land from evil fates,
Lift high her banner fair and free,
And ever guard her liberty.

☆

THE WORKSHOP OF FREEDOM

☆

by Elizabeth Ellen Evans

1954, a senior at Buchtel High School, Akron, Ohio

☆

Hello.
Hello, American.
Hello, my father, my brother, my friend.
We've built a land together.
We've sung and spoken and laughed and cried and thought
and prayed and died together.
And we've taken an idea that's been around for twenty-five
hundred years;
we've taken a word that was only a word and we've
made it a way of life.
We've founded a land on *the freedom of man.*

We started with little but human dreams and an unfailing
will to succeed.
And the world laughed.
The world laughed at our strange idea—
that a man might be free to govern himself, to work and
to pray and to live *as his conscience* demanded.
The conception was old. It had failed before.
The world knew it would fail again.

But not so the brave little land which was built on *the God-
given freedom of man.*

Not so the new-founded Workshop of Freedom.
And the world's amusement turned into amazement, for
the unique idea succeeded!
This Workshop of Freedom—
founded by men with a flame in their hearts
built on the soil of thirteen small colonies facing the sea
her workbenches manned by four million stout-hearted
settlers, giving their best that they and their sons might
stand up as free men—
this Workshop of Freedom has grown and waxed strong.
The thirteen have become forty-eight
the four million, increased forty times
and the best that they gave to the land that they loved
has rendered us great among nations.

And their spirit lives on,
in the mines and the mills
in the farms and the factories
in the power and the prayer
in the laughter and love
in the friendship and faith
that have nourished the Workshop of Freedom.
And American—*we made it work!*
It hasn't been easy, this building a land.
We've paid for our freedom in young men's lives
and in saddened homes
and in broken hearts.
For they were the price of the Workshop of Freedom.
But say that it wasn't worth it?

Walk down the streets of New York and Chicago
  of Cincinnati and San Francisco
  of Pepperton, Georgia, and Roundup, Montana,
  look in the eyes of the people you meet,
  and say that it wasn't worth it.
Hear the high, happy voice of a first grade class singing,
"God bless America. Land that I love . . ."
  Look up at the face of the great, beloved man who sits
    in the Lincoln Memorial
  Walk down a city street swept along by the joyful, ex-
    uberant, heart-warming rush of the last shopping days
    before Christmas
  See the pride in the eyes of a Midwestern farmer on the
    day that his harvest is done
  Tap your foot to the beat of a Dixieland band
  Hear the shout of a thousand kids in a football stadium
    when the home team gets the ball
  See a Star of David and a crucifix and an open Bible side
    by side
And you've seen and you've heard and you've felt in your
  heart the might of the Workshop of Freedom.
Then say that those lives were wasted that ended to make
  and to keep America free!
Say that a life is worth living at all without friendship and
  freedom and faith!

And yet there are men who would take this away.
They stand at the gates to the factories,
  the entrances to the mines,

and they fill the ears of the men who pass by
with their talk of the "common man."
But what a short step from their "common man" to the
common slave!

Tell us these things—if you dare!
Is there one other land on the face of the earth where your
    "common man" can drive home from his work in a car
    of his own to a paper to read and a television set,
        where your "common man" can eat Southern fried
            chicken and chocolate ice cream for his Sunday dinner,
        where his wife can wear nylon stockings and have an
            electric refrigerator?
And then tell us this, you strangers who think you're so
    wise:
        Can a man be a slave when he speaks and he votes and he
            prays as he chooses?
To all who would crumble these freedoms of ours, who
    would undermine our American way of life, we say:
        Show us a hammer and a sickle and we'll show you our
            flag waving high and proud against a cloudless blue
            sky.
        Show us the Communist Manifesto and we'll show you
            our Bill of Rights.
        Show us Malenkov and Stalin and Lenin and we'll show
            you thirty-three presidents, chosen by vote of the peo-
            ple they served . . . and we'll show you a Man on a
            Cross.

And they can't argue back, American!
There's nothing they can say!
The fires of friendship and freedom and faith have been burning too long in our land.
And as long as they burn—as long as those fires burn fervent and bright—there is *nothing* those men can say!

Shake my hand, American.
Shake my hand, my father, my brother, my friend.
Take our hands, all you of the earth who are tired and hungry and cold.
Take our hands, you citizens of the world.
Share with us our friendship and freedom and faith.
They will give you a chance to hold your head high.
They will make you a man.
Come.
Let us walk forward, together and free.

IDEALS ARE LIKE STARS

☆

by Carl Schurz (*1829-1906*)

Civil War General of Volunteers,
Missouri Senator (*1869-75*),
Secretary of the Interior (*1877-81*)

☆

You may tell me that [my] views are visionary, that the destiny of this country is less exalted, that the American people are less great than I think they are or ought to be. I answer, ideals are like stars; you will not succeed in touching them with your hands. But like the seafaring man on the desert of waters, you choose them as your guides, and following them you will reach your destiny.

From a speech in Boston, April, 1859

11

☆

PRAYER FOR AMERICA

☆

by Peter Marshall

Senate Chaplain from
January 6, 1947, to January 25, 1949

☆

Our Father, we pray for this land. We need Thy help in this time of testing and uncertainty, when men who could fight together on the field of battle seem strangely unable to work together around conference tables for peace.

May we begin to see that all true Americanism begins in being Christian; that it can have no other foundation, as it has no other roots.

To Thy glory was this Republic established. For the advancement of the Christian faith did the Founding Fathers give their life's heritage, passed down to us.

We would pray that all over this land there may be a return to the faith of those men and women who trusted in God as they faced the perils and dangers of the frontier, not alone in crossing the continent, in building their cabins, in rearing their families, in eking out a livelihood, but in raising a standard of faith to which men have been willing to repair down through the years.

Thou didst bless their efforts. Thou didst bless America. Thou hast made her rich. Wilt Thou also make her good?

Make us, the citizens of this land, want to do the right things. Make us long to have right attitudes. Help us to be

Christian in our attitudes. Let all that we do and say spring out of understanding hearts.

Make us willing to seek moral objectives together, that in united action this nation may be as resolute for righteousness and peace as she has been for war.

13

PSALM 67

God be merciful unto us, and bless us; *and* cause his face to shine upon us; Selah.

That thy way may be known upon earth, thy saving health among all nations.

Let the people praise thee, O God; let all the people praise thee.

O let the nations be glad and sing for joy: for thou shalt judge the people righteously, and govern the nations upon earth. Selah.

Let the people praise thee, O God; let all the people praise thee.

Then shall the earth yield her increase; *and* God, *even* our own God, shall bless us.

God shall bless us; and all the ends of the earth shall fear him.

O BEAUTIFUL, MY COUNTRY

☆

by Frederick L. Hosmer (1840-1929)

☆

O beautiful, my country!
Be thine a nobler care
Than all thy wealth of commerce,
Thy harvests waving fair;
Be it thy pride to lift up
The manhood of the poor;
Be thou to the oppressed
Fair freedom's open door!

For thee our fathers suffered;
For thee they toiled and prayed;
Upon thy holy altar
Their willing lives they laid.
Thou hast no common birthright,
Grand mem'ries on thee shine;
The blood of pilgrim nations
Commingled flows in thine.

O beautiful, our country!
Round thee in love we draw;
Thine is the grace of freedom,
The majesty of law.

☆

Be righteousness thy scepter,
Justice thy diadem;
And on thy shining forehead
Be peace the crowning gem!

THE STORY OF AMERICA

☆

Robert Gordon Smith

☆

Begin it where you will, and mention all you wish of base or ill, the Story of America is still the record of generations of brave, consecrated men and women who dared to risk their lives and all their worldly goods for the precious right to worship God in their own way, to govern themselves as freeborn children of a Heavenly Father, and to dwell with one another and all mankind in dignity, mutual helpfulness, and love.

☆

LANDING OF THE PILGRIM FATHERS

☆

by Felicia Hemans (*1793-1835*)

☆

The breaking waves dashed high
On the stern and rock-bound coast,
And the woods, against a stormy sky,
Their giant branches tossed;

And the heavy night hung dark
The hills and waters o'er,
When a band of exiles moored their bark
On the wild New England shore.

Not as the conqueror comes,
They, the true-hearted, came:
Not with the roll of the stirring drums,
And the trumpet that sings of fame;

Not as the flying come,
In silence and in fear—
They shook the depths of the desert's gloom
With their hymns of lofty cheer.

Amidst the storm they sang,
And the stars heard, and the sea;
And the sounding aisles of the dim woods rang
To the anthem of the free!

The ocean-eagle soared
From his nest by the white wave's foam,
And the rocking pines of the forest roared:
This was their welcome home!

There were men with hoary hair
Amidst that pilgrim band;
Why have they come to wither there,
Away from their childhood's land?

There was woman's fearless eye,
Lit by her deep love's truth;
There was manhood's brow, serenely high,
And the fiery heart of youth.

What sought they thus afar?
Bright jewels of the mine?
The wealth of seas, the spoils of war?
They sought a faith's pure shrine!

Aye, call it holy ground,
The soil where first they trod!
They have left unstained what there they found:
Freedom to worship God.

19

☆

THE LORD WAS THEIR SHEPHERD

☆

John Hancock Mutual Life Insurance Company

1950, 1951

☆

The first thing they did when they got off the ship was to kneel down under the open sky and thank God. That was why they had come here . . . to meet God in the way they thought right.

It was a simple, manly way they had with Him. Each man seeking His presence, reading His word, listening to His voice, trying to understand His way and to live by it. Each man a free man, responsible to God.

It was not only on Sundays, or in church alone, that they thought of Him, but always and everywhere. They felt that the world was God's house, and they walked reverently in it, and they tried to remember to live by His ways.

So it was that when they wrote a Declaration of Independence, in that fateful moment of making themselves a nation, they called upon Him to behold the justice of what they were about to do.

And when they met to draw up a Constitution, governing how Americans should behave towards each other, they prayed for guidance from the Highest Lawgiver of all.

And from that day to this, when we come together to make a solemn public decision, we take a moment to ask

God to make our minds wise, and our hearts good, and our motives pure.

Surely there never was a better country to find God in. Out on the open coast, where the ocean stirs forever and ever, always changing and always the same; on the prairies, where the grass blows and ripens and dies and is born again; in the wild, high mountains and in the silent desert—everywhere under this wide sky the feeling comes: *Someone has been here. Someone has made this beautiful for me. Someone expects me to be worthy of this.*

Someone expects me to be worthy . . . Through most of our history we have lived with that faith. And only as long as we believe it, and go on living by it, will we be secure.

☆

THE FOUNDATIONS OF FREEDOM

☆

by Gordon Fox

*From an address delivered on Engineers' Day, 1955, at the
University of Wisconsin*

☆

To worship God according to their own convictions, a little band of Pilgrims braved the tempestuous sea and settled on the New England coast. There they established a colony. More important, they established a principle, a tradition, that the adoration of God and the emulation of Christ should form the cornerstone upon which to build the glorious edifice of this nation.

Thus the first and foremost caisson of the foundation which undergirds our land is a concept of recognition, of veneration and of adherence to moral values, a deep-seated conviction that no system of organization of human relationships can be fundamentally right if that system does not have its roots in a moral code based on the tenets of religion.

Another great principle forms the second caisson of the foundation upon which has been built America's preeminence. It is the principle of recognition of the dignity of the individual person and the sanctity of the individual soul. It is a part of this concept that every man has a direct and equal relationship with God, that no man has power over another "by divine right" and that life is granted to each of us as a stewardship in which our major mission is to employ, to the full, the special talents with which we are, in varied measure, by our Creator, endowed.

The founders of our nation pioneered the principle that every citizen is vested with God-given rights and charged with God-given responsibilities, that he is free to make his own decisions and to establish his own personal pattern of life so long as he does not trespass upon the equal privileges of others. It is a corollary of this principle that government has no sovereign rights and no inherent functions other than those voluntarily and specifically delegated to it by its citizens.

The American Constitution is based on the postulate that man derives his rights from God, that to secure and protect those rights, it is expedient that he delegate specific powers and functions to the State, that within these prescribed limits, man is, by choice, accountable to the State, but that, in all other areas, he is accountable only to God.

The Declaration of Independence, the Constitution of the United States, and the Bill of Rights are among the world's greatest documents, because they emphasize, as never before in history, the prerogatives of the citizen as contrasted with the powers of government. Our Constitution was designed to protect the freedom of the minimal minority, one person. The idea of the inalienable rights of the individual citizen is the fundamental spirit of the American tradition of government.

The third great principle, the third caisson supporting the stupendous superstructure of our United States, is the principle of dispersed powers, decentralized decisions and distributed authority. Our revolutionary forebears, conversant with the history of man's long struggle for freedom, and having themselves tasted the bitter oppression of absolute power, sought to insure for all time that no segment of government should attain a position of domination. To this end they retained in the people the prime source of authority. They vested in the states control over local affairs; representatives of the states, in turn, delegated to the federal government only limited powers in matters pertaining to the common defense and the general welfare. They provided in both state and federal governments separate legislative, executive, and judicial bodies and instituted a system of checks and balances aimed to prevent the dominance of one of these over another.

Our governmental structure bears the evidence of a canny comprehension of the dangers inherent in any concentration of governmental authority and indicates a firm determination to forestall such an eventuality in America.

The concept of the primacy of the individual, the concept of God-given rights, the concept of limited, delegated governmental powers and dispersed dominion, these are the attributes of individualism; they are the hallmarks of freedom; they constitute our legacy of liberty.

FOR ALL MEN

☆

by Daniel Webster

From an address marking the completion of
Bunker Hill Monument, June 17, 1843

☆

America has proved that it is practicable to elevate the mass of mankind—that portion which in Europe is called the laboring, or lower class—to raise them to self-respect, to make them competent to act a part in the great right and great duty of self-government; and she has proved that this may be done by education and the diffusion of knowledge. She holds out an example, a thousand times more encouraging than ever was presented before, to those nine-tenths of the human race who are born without hereditary fortune or hereditary rank.

THE AMERICAN WAY OF LIFE

Credo of Freedoms Foundation, Valley Forge

POLITICAL AND ECONOMIC RIGHTS WHICH PROTECT THE DIGNITY AND FREEDOM OF THE INDIVIDUAL:

Right to worship God in one's own way.
Right to free speech and press.
Right to assemble.
Right to petition for grievances.
Right to privacy in our homes.
Right of habeas corpus—no excessive bail.
Right to trial by jury—innocent till proved guilty.
Right to move about freely at home and abroad.
Right to own private property.
Right to work in callings and localities of our choice.
Right to bargain with our employers.
Right to go into business, compete, make a profit.
Right to bargain for goods and services in a free market.
Right to contract about our affairs.
Right to the service of government as a protector and referee.
Right to freedom from "arbitrary" government regulation and control.

CONSTITUTIONAL GOVERNMENT DESIGNED TO SERVE THE
PEOPLE

FUNDAMENTAL BELIEF IN GOD

To maintain the American Way of Life and pass it intact to
succeeding generations is the *responsibility* of every *true
American.*

THE LONG VIEW OF PETER BOS
☆
by Wessel Smitter
1948
☆

In 1869 Peter Bos gave up his home, his friends, and a good job as head gardener on a large estate in Holland, and made the long trip to America. In his heart he cherished what is still the essence of the American Dream—an abiding faith in the individual's right and ability to take a part in shaping his own and his country's future.

With his young wife and two small children, Peter finally reached the village of Holland, Michigan, where he had friends. But he was not interested in town life; he had come to America to become a farmer. Also, he saw that the town customs were those the people had brought from the old country. The women wore clothes made from imported Dutch woolens; the men wore wooden shoes that they removed before entering the house. That was all right for those who wanted to remain Hollanders, but Peter had determined to become an American.

Near Manistee, a lumber town in the pine country of northern Michigan, cut-over land could be had for ten dollars an acre. There Peter found an eighty-acre plot where the soil was deep and rich. It lay in the midst of a slash-covered wilderness, two miles from the nearest neighbor. The pine stumps were unusually large, but Peter reasoned that the land must be good to have produced such gigantic trees. He bought the tract.

With the help of his wife he built a two-room house and a barn. He bought a horse, a cow, chickens, a light wagon, and a few hand tools, nearly exhausting his savings. That summer the family gathered quantities of wild blackberries and blueberries and sold them to the hotel-keeper in the village and the lumber schooners on Lake Michigan. It was the first money Peter had earned in the new country, and with some of it he bought a Bible.

"It's in English—we can't read it!" his wife said. "Besides, we have already a Dutch Bible. What good are two Bibles?"

That evening after supper he showed her. Every day, after each meal, Peter read aloud from the Dutch Bible; that was the old custom. Now, as he opened the Dutch Bible, he gave his wife the new one and bade her follow the reading. At first it was difficult, but soon she began to learn rapidly because she was so familiar with the contents.

Then they took turn about, so that Peter might also learn English. He had already taken out his first citizenship papers and he hoped that in five years, when he would become a full citizen, they would have learned the new language well enough to put the old Bible away. They did it in three years.

During the first winter Peter worked in a lumber camp at twenty dollars a month, while his wife did the chores on the farm. Saturday nights he walked fourteen miles through the deep snow to spend Sunday with his family, and started back at two o'clock Monday morning.

In the spring he tackled the stumps, of which there were hundreds. But when planting time came not more than a

half acre had been cleared, only enough for the garden;
the field crops—corn, potatoes, peas, and barley—had to
be planted among the stumps. That summer Peter's wife
was pregnant and she was unable to help him much.

One day a man from a nearby lumber camp hurried into
the clearing. "The woods are on fire!" he shouted. "It's
coming this way. Get to the lake!"

Quickly Peter and his wife loaded their few precious
belongings on the wagon along with a crate of chickens,
and, with the two children on the seat between them and
the cow tied behind, they started the bumpy journey over
twelve miles of rough logging roads to Lake Michigan.

As darkness came, the red glare of the raging flames
filled the eastern sky behind them. At times the fire appeared to be gaining, but twice Peter stopped, took the
lantern, made his way through dim trails, and carried the
warning to others.

On the sandy beach near Manistee harbor they found
other families who had fled to safety. Peter's wife fed the
children and put them to sleep in the wagon. Then she said,
"Peter, the pains have started. I think you had better go
into town for the doctor."

That night, just before dawn, in a rough shelter made
with blankets, their third child, a girl, was born.

The following day reports of other fires began coming
in. Peshtigo, with a loss of 600 lives, was wiped out; Holland had burned to the ground. When Peter walked back
to his clearing to see what was left of the farm, the house
was gone, but, miraculously, the barn had escaped.

People who had lost their homes were fighting for space

on departing lumber schooners, but Peter would not join them. He felt that to do so would be to break faith with the things America stood for. "We are going to stay," he said. "Here we have a little piece of America in which to send out our roots."

Shortly after the fire, credit he obtained from the lumber company enabled Peter to build a new house. In the fall he purchased another horse and that winter he worked his team in the lumber camp at sixty dollars a month.

The next spring, with the help of my grandfather, Peter designed and built a stump puller. Peter and his wife cleared six acres and the crops flourished until late August, when a killing frost ruined the potatoes and corn. One of Peter's neighbors, his entire crop gone, gave up the struggle. "The land is good for nothing," he complained, "except for growing trees. You would see that if you were not a stubborn Dutchman."

Peter told his wife what the man had said. "Good for nothing except growing trees." Maybe this was so, but what kind of trees?

In the old country Peter had experimented with budding and grafting. Now the answer to the question evolved out of his own observations. He had never seen wild cherry trees like those that grew in the surrounding countryside. Raising cherry trees that bore commercial fruit—that might be the answer!

That fall Peter told the owner of the lumber company about his plan for raising cherries and his need for help in carrying out a long series of experiments. The lumberman agreed to finance Peter's experiments to the extent of $500 a year for five years.

The following spring Peter planted 400 young cherry trees, of every variety obtainable from nurserymen. Many did not survive the first winter, and these weak varieties were discarded.

The second year more trees were planted, and also hundreds of wild-cherry seeds to provide healthy root stock. When the young seedlings came up, Peter cut off their tops and grafted young buds from commercial trees onto them.

These were hard years for Peter Bos. The annual $500 was not enough to carry on the experiments and supply even the simple wants of the family. To get cash he worked with the road crews.

After a long process of elimination and selection he found several varieties of cherries that were able to withstand the severe winter temperatures. Success finally came with the grafting of buds from a variety of commercial sour cherry to the hardy root stock of the wild native cherry, and in 1880 the young trees came into bearing. Peter distributed 800 trees, half his entire stock, to friends and neighbors.

Today, largely because of Peter Bos's experiments, the Grand Traverse Bay district of Michigan is famous the world over. It produces about 90,000,000 pounds of sour cherries a year—more than any other region in the country.

When I knew Peter Bos, after the turn of the century, I was only a kid in knee breeches. At that time he was the owner of a fine up-to-date orchard, a major stockholder in the district's first cherry cannery, owned a large nursery, and held the office of county supervisor. No longer young, he had turned his business affairs over to his two capable sons.

America, for him, continued to be an exciting phenomenon; being an American citizen, a cherished responsibility.

After an absence of twenty years I visited the old neighborhood. Peter Bos was no longer alive, but his influence was. I talked with the daughter who was born at the time of the great fire.

"I was the only one of the three children who went to college," she said. "The family had to sacrifice for my education. Later, when I got a job teaching school, I tried to repay the debt. But Father said, 'You don't owe it to us; you owe it to the country that built the school and hired the teachers. I expect you to pay it all back.' "

"Did you?" I asked.

"I tried," she said. But she did not tell me what I already knew—that for years she was superintendent of education in a neighboring county, and that through her own sacrifices and efforts every school in that district had a library.

There are ten grandchildren. Three are teachers, one a research engineer, one a widely known surgeon. Another, a county agricultural agent, took me out to the old Bos farm, now a part of the Manistee National Forest. The buildings were gone, and so were the cherry trees. But there were magnificent white pines, fifty feet tall, grown from seedlings Peter Bos had set out when he realized that otherwise Michigan's lumber industry would soon end.

"My grandfather held to the long view," said my guide, pointing to the sweeping pines. "He was proud of his citizenship, and did something about it."

I spent a day with another grandson, a university professor home on vacation, in the neighboring town of Traverse City. The town was gay with flags and bunting in celebration of the big event of the year—the National Cherry Festival.

"Your grandfather would have enjoyed this," I said as he watched the parade.

"Maybe he did," my companion answered, and for a moment the answer puzzled me. Then I remembered Peter Bos's long view and saw that this, too, may well have been part of his dream.

SENATE PRAYER

☆

by Peter Marshall
January 5, 1949

☆

Our Father in heaven, give us the long view of our work and our world.

Help us to see that it is better to fail in a cause that will ultimately succeed than to succeed in a cause that will ultimately fail.

Guide us how to work and then teach us how to wait. O Lord, we pray in the name of Jesus, who was never in a hurry. Amen.

☆

AN AMERICAN PROVERB

☆

Anonymous

☆

Hats off to the past;
Coats off to the future.

WORLD-WIDE CHALLENGE

☆

by W. Averell Harriman

From "No Depression Necessary,"
American Legion Magazine, *June, 1947*

☆

In Moscow during World War II, a member of the United States Embassy staff was in a Russian store waiting in line to buy some food. Just in front of her was a man who asked for four ounces of butter. The clerk cut a piece from a large slab and placed it on the scale. The needle pointed exactly to the four-ounce mark. The man looked at the clerk very pleased, and said in Russian, "Oh, that is just like American accuracy." He meant that the clerk weighed the piece perfectly.

To him the word "American" stood for precision and excellence. If that impression of us is true in Russia, it is even more true in other countries in which I have traveled and worked. They expect us to be the best.

☆

TO RENEW THE SPIRIT THAT BUILT OUR COUNTRY

☆

Have
Faith
in God
in Ourselves
in Our Fellow Men
in Freedom

IN THE FAITH WE PLACE IN GOD . . . in ourselves as individuals . . . in our fellow men and . . . in Freedom—rests the future of our nation!

The faith of our country's founders was a sturdy and simple faith.

They believed in the Power which sustains through any crisis.

Upheld and guided by that Power, they believed in their own strength to do, to achieve, to build.

And, thus sustained and fortified, they believed that Freedom was more than an abstract dream; they made it an accomplished fact.

This Freedom is our children's birthright—ours to hand on to them and to their children—undiminished, undespoiled.

This is a sacred trust—one in which we must not fail.

Yet these are troubled times. *What can we do?*

We can do as those before us did . . . renew the spirit that built our country.

We need . . . Faith in God, Who answers prayer . . .
Faith in ourselves, and in our work . . . Faith in our
fellow men, their courage and their honesty . . . Faith
in Freedom . . . and in its strength!

When we have done these things—and only then—can
we be secure in the knowledge that our children will be
free and our country safe.

We must not fail.

Texas and Pacific Railway Company, 1952

☆

PRAYER IN CARPENTERS' HALL,
PHILADELPHIA

☆

by Dr. Jacob Duche

Given at the first meeting of the
First Continental Congress, September, 1774

☆

O Lord, our Heavenly Father, high and mighty King of
Kings, Lord of Lords, who dost from Thy throne behold
all the dwellers upon the earth, and reignest with power
supreme and uncontrolled over all kingdoms, empires, and
governments, look down in mercy, we beseech Thee, upon
these American States who have fled to Thee from the rod
of the oppressor, and thrown themselves upon Thy gracious protection, desiring to be henceforth dependent only
upon Thee.

To Thee have they appealed for the righteousness of
their cause. To Thee do they now look up for that countenance and support which Thou alone canst give. Take
them, therefore, Heavenly Father, under Thy nurturing
care. Give them wisdom in council and valor in the field.
Defeat the malicious designs of our cruel adversaries. Convince them of the unrighteousness of their cause, and if
they still persist in their sanguinary purpose, O let the
voice of Thine own unerring justice, sounding in their
hearts, constrain them to drop their weapons of war from
their unnerved hands in the day of battle.

Be Thou present, O Lord of Wisdom, and direct the
Council of the honorable Assembly. Enable them to settle

things upon the best and surest foundation, that the scene of blood may speedily be closed; that order, harmony, and peace may effectually be restored, and truth and justice, religion and piety, prevail and flourish amongst Thy people.

Preserve the health of their bodies, the vigor of their minds. Shower down upon them, and the millions they here represent, such temporal blessings as Thou seest expedient for them in this world and crown them with everlasting glory in the world to come. All this we ask in the name and through the merits of Jesus Christ, Thy Son, our Savior. Amen.

THE WAR INEVITABLE

☆

by Patrick Henry

From an address to the
Virginia House of Burgesses, March 23, 1775

☆

They tell us, Sir, that we are weak, unable to cope with so formidable an adversary. But when shall we be stronger? Will it be the next week, or the next year? Will it be when we are totally disarmed, and when a British guard shall be stationed in every house? Shall we gather strength by irresolution and inaction? Shall we acquire the means of effectual resistance by lying supinely on our backs, and hugging the delusive phantom of hope, until our enemies shall have bound us hand and foot? Sir, we are not weak, if we make a proper use of those means which the God of nature hath placed in our power.

Three millions of People, armed in the holy cause of liberty, and in such a country as that which we possess, are invincible by any force which our enemy can send against us. Besides, Sir, we shall not fight our battles alone. There is a just God who presides over the destinies of Nations, and who will raise up friends to fight our battles for us. The battle, Sir, is not to the strong alone; it is to the vigilant, the active, the brave. Besides, Sir, we have no election. If we were base enough to desire it, it is now too late to retire from the contest. There is no retreat but in submission and slavery! Our chains are forged! Their clanking may be heard on the plains of Boston! The war is inevitable; and let it come! I repeat, Sir, let it come!

It is in vain, Sir, to extenuate the matter. Gentlemen may cry, Peace, Peace!—but there is no peace. The war is actually begun! The next gale that sweeps from the North will bring to our ears the clash of resounding arms! Our brethren are already in the field! Why stand we here idle? What is it that Gentlemen wish? What would they have? Is life so dear, or peace so sweet, as to be purchased at the price of chains and slavery? Forbid it, Almighty God! I know not what course others may take; but as for me, give me liberty or give me death!

PSALM 46

God *is* our refuge and strength, a very present help in trouble.

Therefore will not we fear, though the earth be removed, and though the mountains be carried into the midst of the sea;

Though the waters thereof roar *and* be troubled, *though* the mountains shake with the swelling thereof. Selah.

There is a river, the streams whereof shall make glad the city of God, the holy *place* of the tabernacles of the most High.

God *is* in the midst of her; she shall not be moved: God shall help her, *and that* right early.

The heathen raged, the kingdoms were moved: he uttered his voice, the earth melted.

The Lord of hosts *is* with us; the God of Jacob *is* our refuge. Selah.

Come, behold the works of the Lord, what desolations he hath made in the earth.

He maketh wars to cease unto the end of the earth; he breaketh the bow, and cutteth the spear in sunder; he burneth the chariot in the fire.

Be still, and know that I *am* God: I will be exalted among the heathen, I will be exalted in the earth.

The Lord of hosts *is* with us; the God of Jacob *is* our refuge. Selah.

☆

LOVE OF LIBERTY

☆

by George Washington
From *Farewell Address, September 17, 1796*

☆

Interwoven as is the love of liberty with every ligament of your hearts, no recommendation of mine is necessary to fortify or confirm the attachment.

TO THE AMERICAN TROOPS BEFORE THE BATTLE OF LONG ISLAND

☆

by George Washington
From General Orders of August 13, 1776

☆

The enemy's whole reinforcement is now arrived, so that an attack must, and will soon be made; the General therefore again repeats his earnest request, that every officer, and soldier, will have his arms and ammunition in good order, keep within his quarters and encampment, as much as possible; be ready for action at a moment's call; and when called to it, remember that liberty, property, life, and honor are all at stake; upon their courage and conduct rest the hopes of their bleeding and insulted country; that their wives, children, and parents expect safety from them only, and that we have every reason to expect Heaven will crown with success so just a cause.

The enemy will endeavor to intimidate by show and appearance, but remember how they have been repulsed, on various occasions, by a few brave Americans; their cause is bad; their men are conscious of it, and if opposed with firmness, and coolness, at their first onset, with our advantage of Works, and knowledge of our ground, Victory is most assuredly ours.

☆

WASHINGTON

☆

by Nancy Byrd Turner

☆

He played by the river when he was young,
He raced with the rabbits along the hills,
He fished for minnows, and climbed and swung,
And hooted back at the whippoorwills.
Strong and slender and tall he grew
And then, one morning, the bugles blew.

Over the hills the summons came,
Over the river's shining rim.
He said that the bugles called his name,
He knew that his country needed him,
And he answered, "Coming!" and marched away
For many a night and many a day.

Perhaps when the marches were hot and long
He'd think of the river flowing by,
Or, camping under the winter sky,
Would hear the whippoorwill's far-off song.
At work, at play, and in peace or strife,
He loved America all his life!

THE MOTHER OF INDEPENDENCE

☆

by *Kincaid Neil*

1959

☆

"I long to hear that you have declared an independency," wrote Abigail Adams to her husband in 1776. "And by the way, in the new code of law. . . . . I desire you would remember the ladies, and be more generous and favorable to them than your ancestors. Do not put such unlimited power into the hands of the husbands. Remember, all men would be tyrants if they could."

It was the first voice raised in America toward bettering the lot of women under the new constitution. And Abigail Adams—wife of one President and mother of another, the bold feminine symbol of the whole Revolutionary spirit—was a woman whose words had weight.

"If particular care is not paid to the ladies," she added humorously, "we are determined to foment a rebellion, and will not hold ourselves bound by any laws in which we have no voice or representation."

Her husband John Adams, the nation's second president, was a crotchety and unbending old Puritan who had most of the talent and none of the tact of his magnanimous predecessor. But the strength of Abigail's love, her graceful, coaxing letters during their long separations humanized John Adams and helped him forge the important decisions that were building the nation.

They had been apart almost constantly for two years—

John thrashing out pre-revolutionary matters at Philadelphia; Abigail remaining at home near Boston because it
was less expensive to live there. "I dare not express to you,
at three hundred miles' distance, how ardently I long for
your return," she wrote. ". . . . . absence knows not how
to brook further restraint, but will break forth and flow
through my pen. May the like sensations enter thy breast."

When hostilities broke out in Boston, Abigail was in the
thick of it. It's from this period that we derive the famous picture of her, children clinging to her skirts (one
of whom, John Quincy, would become sixth President
of the United States), watching the bombardment of Boston from Dorchester Heights. Later pictures showed her
hanging up the Presidential wash to dry in the great unfinished East Room of the White House.

She was an aristocratic soul, and when, at the age of
nineteen, she married the Harvard-educated son of a Brain-
tree farmer, her relatives stormily insisted that she had
married beneath her station. Was she not the daughter of
a Congregational minister and product of an impressive
line of New England preachers? Was she not related by
marriage to half the prominent families in the Boston area?
But Abigail was never considered a beauty, and portraits
of her show a rather stern, elongated, patrician face. She
was antic and amusing, however, and possessed the kind
of charming good sense that ambitious men often seek in
their wives.

Her story is the eternal saga of woman in war: loneli-
ness, deprivation, the rearing of children while the head of
the house is away.

"I feel very differently at the approach of spring from what I did a month ago," she wrote her husband. "We knew not then whether we could plant or sow with safety, whether when we had tilled we could reap the fruits of our own industry, whether we could rest in our own cottages or whether we should be driven from the seacoast to seek shelter in the wilderness; but now we feel a temporary peace, and the poor fugitives are returning to their deserted habitations."

But at the height of her deprivation, she was concerned that the "new code of law" insure her sex a place of dignity in the new nation:

"That your sex are naturally tyrannical," she wrote to John, "is a truth so thoroughly established as to admit of no dispute; but such of you as wish to be happy willingly give up the harsh title of master for the more tender and endearing one of friend. . . . . Men of sense in all ages abhor those customs which treat us only as the vassals of your sex; regard us then as being placed by Providence under your protection, and in imitation of the Supreme Being make use of that power only for our happiness."

That was Abigail—mother of statesmen and of independence for women everywhere.

51

☆

THE GREATEST GLORY

☆

by William Havard

English actor and playwright, 1710-78

☆

The greatest glory of a free-born people
Is to transmit that freedom to their children.

From Regulus, *Act V, Sc. 4*

AND THEN OUR FREEDOM BEGAN

☆

by Hugh Scott

1951

☆

Outside the State House, starting just beyond the imperfect glass of its small-paned windows, Philadelphia was heavy with summer languor. Roses, bright in June, now nodded indolently and dropped their petals to brick pavements still wet with the forenoon's rain. Beyond Broad Street the knee-deep meadows were murmurous with bees, and everywhere else early July lassitude softened the voice of the Colonial city.

But inside the State House the atmosphere held some of January's chill of doubt. There the Continental Congress was irritably slapping at horseflies from a nearby stable, and just as irritably editing the Declaration of Independence which Thomas Jefferson had written out so carefully in the second-floor-front study of his lodgings at Seventh and Market (then High) Streets. So far the delegates had cut nearly a quarter of the Virginian's careful copy, while he squirmed silently in his seat.

Carefully shifting his gouty leg, Benjamin Franklin leaned over to the sandy-haired young man beside him. "You shouldn't be upset," he said gently. "I remember when a friend of mine wanted a sign made. The sign started out as John Thompson, Hatter, Makes and Sells Hats for Ready Money, with the picture of a hat . . ."

Jefferson listened politely, his unfocused gaze shifting

from the silver inkstand on Hancock's desk to the burly shoulders of Ben Harrison. He wished there were some way of keeping horseflies out of the State House, and that Dr. Franklin would get to the point of his story.

"When Thompson showed the sign to some of his friends," Franklin continued, "each had a suggestion. One objected to the tautology of *hatter* and *makes hats;* another saw no need to include *for Ready Money.* A third pointed out that it didn't matter who made the hats so long as they were good. And, in the end, the sign just had the name *John Thompson* and a picture of a hat."

The connection between the hatter's sign and the Declaration over which he had perspired during much of June seemed remote to Jefferson. But he smiled at the story. He couldn't help liking Franklin, and he knew the Pennsylvanian was just trying to make him feel better.

Still, he thought, the delegates might have left in those paragraphs on slavery; he had liked them. Congress, although Jefferson didn't know it, was exhibiting a love of brevity that would characterize few of its sessions in the future.

Jefferson hadn't objected to the dozen-odd brief changes made by Franklin in his copy. After all, Franklin was on the five-man committee assigned to draw up the declaration, even if all the writing had been done by himself.

One of Franklin's changes was especially good, changing "a" to "one" in the first sentence so that it read: "When in the course of human events it becomes necessary for one people to dissolve the political bands which have connected them with another, and to assume among the powers of the earth, the separate and equal station to which the Laws of Nature and of Nature's God entitle them, a decent respect to the opinions of mankind requires that they should declare the causes which impel them to the separation."

Franklin also had capitalized *Nature's God* and changed *threatened separation* to *the separation,* which Jefferson agreed was logical.

Abruptly the tall Virginian straightened his angular figure in his chair. These things, after all, were relatively unimportant compared with the larger question: Would the Congress as a whole approve the Declaration? It was true, he reflected, the general idea already had been approved. But this was more formal, more definite. It would bring to the delegates' minds more directly Franklin's wry comment: "Now we must all hang together or most assuredly we shall hang separately." Franklin's humor, Jefferson thought, sometimes was unfortunate.

The idea of independence, he knew, had many critics and they were well armed with realistic arguments. You could hear them in the shops along High Street and in the counting houses near the river, in the markets and on the docks. "Where," they asked, "are we going to get an army to stand up to the British regulars? Where are we going to get a navy to defend a thousand miles of coastline? Where are we going to get factories to turn out cannon and powder and shot? Are not many other British subjects taxed without representation? Why can't our differences with Britain be settled by legal means?"

"American independence," one man had written recently, "is as illusory, ruinous, and impractical as a liberal reconciliation with Great Britain is right, honorable, and expedient."

There were two things wrong with this last argument, Jefferson thought. First, England had shown no desire for a liberal reconciliation; second, the colonies had moved far beyond the point where a few soft words would soothe their feelings.

Moderation might be sensible—at least, he amended, it might have been sensible, but it certainly wasn't popular. Not with Sam Adams stirring up Massachusetts and Patrick Henry doing the same thing in Virginia. It was odd that the North and South colonies should share the most violence of feeling. The middle colonies were only lukewarm. New York, he knew, wouldn't vote for the Declaration, and Pennsylvania and Maryland would be divided.

Most of the men in the room were basically conservative. At least a dozen were lawyers. Others were merchants and farmers and doctors, solid men, almost all well-to-do, and therefore with a lot to lose.

Like many other delegates, Jefferson often wished he could see into the future. Fortunately for the United States this was impossible. For many of the men who risked their lives by signing Jefferson's Declaration were to suffer for it. Fourteen signers would lose their homes and personal property during the war. At least nine would be forced to flee and hide. Four would die from hardships and overwork during the Revolution. Two would be wounded in battle and five taken prisoner. One would be killed in a duel, another poisoned.

Jefferson, at thirty-three, was one of the youngest signers; Franklin was the oldest, seventy. Forty-eight were American born; the other eight had been born in the British Isles. Twenty-one were university graduates, and most of the rest had received adequate private schooling. Charles Carroll of Maryland was the richest man in America. John Hancock was the wealthiest man in New England, and Philip Livingston was called the richest man in New York. The single really poor signer was Samuel Adams of Boston. His father had left him a prosperous brewing business, but he had let it fall apart while busy working for independence. When Adams left for Philadelphia his friends had to give him a new suit of clothes and a purse of money.

Jefferson, who had nearly ten thousand acres of land in Virginia, was one of the more affluent delegates. He had driven up from Monticello in mid-May, taking eight days for the journey, and had rented the entire second floor of Hyman Gratz's new brick house for his stay in Philadelphia. Jefferson used the front room as his sitting-room-study. There he had his specially made desk and, something quite unusual at that time, a swivel chair. There, too, after he was named to the committee, he wrote the Declaration.

On the committee with Jefferson were Benjamin Franklin, John Adams, Roger Sherman, and Robert R. Livingston. All gave advice, and Franklin and Adams carefully went over the finished document before it was submitted to Congress. But it was Jefferson who did all the actual writing.

Franklin, perhaps, was as well fitted for the job, but he had made a rule not to write anything that would be edited. Jefferson, being younger, was more amenable. At the same time he mixed a sound knowledge of history, law, and government with a deep faith in the destiny of his country. But even Jefferson couldn't dash off such a document. Instead he ground it out, slowly and painfully, and his early draft is riddled with changes and corrections. Added to his own changes in the final document were those of Franklin, Adams, and the harsher cuts and corrections of the Congress.

Between sessions of labor on the Declaration, Jefferson, always curious and usually rather seriously inquisitive, managed to see quite a bit of Philadelphia. Just before he started writing the document, he paid a shilling to see a monkey, and, as usual, neatly noted the expense in his account book. He bought toys and a doll and paid twenty-seven shillings for fiddle strings.

Later, while he was writing the Declaration, he paid a shilling sixpence for a new pencil, seven shillings sixpence for a map, and two shillings sixpence for a quire of hand-made, laid paper, with the singularly appropriate water-mark, *Pro Patria Eiusque Libertate*. Today a single sheet of that paper holding Jefferson's much-stroked-out first draft would be worth several thousand dollars if only as an indication of how the Declaration developed.

In one sentence, which the Congress never saw, Jefferson had written, "This is too much to be borne even by relations: enough then be it to say, we are now done with them." Jefferson himself substituted a more gentle sentence, and Congress wisely threw it all out.

In the end, although Congress had fussed a great deal over phrases, done enough cutting to reduce the length of the Declaration by a quarter, and thoroughly irritated Jefferson, the Declaration of Independence was approved rather quietly. It has been suggested that the activities of the horseflies speeded the process; actually, it was late in the day before the United States was thus formally born.

Philadelphia's reaction to the adoption of the Declaration was notable only for its modesty. The complete document didn't appear in a newspaper until the sixth of July. It was first read to the public on the eighth of July, and it was signed by most of the delegates on the second of August. The city, at that time, was more interested in the process of the Revolutionary War, already well under way, than in the legislative formalities of Independence.

But to Jefferson, at least, July 4, 1776, was a great day. In his lodgings that night he leafed through his notes, repeating some of the phrases whose sound he best liked: "We hold these truths to be self-evident, that all men are created equal, that they are endowed by their Creator with certain unalienable Rights, that among these are Life, Liberty, and the pursuit of Happiness. . . . ." Then, pushing the papers aside, he swung his chair around and looked out into the soft summer darkness.

Below him on High Street the lantern of a watchman

spread a dim circle of light on a brick house front. A horse whinnied in a nearby stable and out beyond Eighth Street a dog barked. Then the city was silent.

"It could be a great nation," Jefferson said. "And it will be—if we learn to pull together."

LIBERTY MUST BE EARNED

☆

by Charles C. Colton (1780-1832)

English clergyman

☆

Liberty will not descend to a people; a people must raise themselves to liberty; it is a blessing that must be earned before it can be enjoyed.

From Lacon, *1820*

I AM WHAT YOU MAKE ME
(*The Flag Speaks*)

☆

by *Franklin K. Lane*
published during World War I

☆

I am whatever you make me, nothing more.

I am your belief in yourself, your dream of what a people may become.

I live a changing life, a life of moods and passions, of heart-breaks and tired muscles.

Sometimes I am strong with pride, when workmen do an honest piece of work,

Sometimes I droop, for then purpose has gone from me, and cynically I play the coward;

But always I am all that you hope to be, and have the courage to try for.

I am song and fear, struggle and panic, and ennobling hope.

I am the day's work of the weakest man, and the largest dream of the most daring.

I am what you make me, nothing more.

I swing before your eyes as a bright gleam of color,

A symbol of yourself,

A pictured suggestion of that big thing which makes this nation.

My stars and stripes are your dream and your labors,
They are bright with cheer, brilliant with courage, firm
with faith,
Because you have made them so out of your hearts.

A DECLARATION

☆

by the Representatives of the United States of America in Congress Assembled

(*July 4, 1776*)

☆

When, in the course of human events, it becomes necessary for one people to dissolve the political bands which have connected them with another, and to assume among the powers of the earth, the separate and equal station to which the Laws of Nature and Nature's God entitle them, a decent respect to the opinions of mankind requires that they should declare the causes which impel them to the separation.

We hold these truths to be self-evident, that all men are created equal, that they are endowed by their Creator with certain unalienable Rights, that among these are Life, Liberty, and the Pursuit of Happiness. That to secure these Rights, Governments are instituted among Men, deriving their just powers from the consent of the governed. That, whenever any form of Government becomes destructive of these ends, it is the Right of the People to alter or to abolish it, and to institute new Government, laying its foundation on such principles and organizing its powers in such form, as to them shall seem most likely to effect their Safety and Happiness.

Prudence, indeed, will dictate that Governments long established should not be changed for light and transient causes; and accordingly all experience hath shewn, that mankind are more disposed to suffer, while evils are sufferable, than to right themselves by abolishing the forms to which they are accustomed. But when a long train of abuses and usurpations, pursuing invariably the same object, evidence a design to reduce them under absolute Despotism, it is their right, it is their duty, to throw off such Government, and to provide new Guards for their future security.

Such has been the patient sufferance of these Colonies, and such is now the necessity which constrains them to alter their former Systems of Government. The history of the present King of Great Britain is a history of repeated injuries and usurpation, all having, in direct object, the establishment of an absolute Tyranny over these States. To prove this, let facts be submitted to a candid world.

[Following is a list of general and specific grievances against the king, a statement of the colonies' unsuccessful attempts to redress these grievances without separation from England, and a conclusion that separation is necessary.]

We, therefore, the Representatives of the United States of America, in General Congress, Assembled, appealing to the Supreme Judge of the world for the rectitude of our intentions, do, in the Name, and by Authority of the good People of these Colonies, solemnly publish and declare, That these United Colonies are, and of Right ought to be Free and Independent States; that they are Absolved from all Allegiance to the British Crown, and that all political connection between them and the State of Great Britain, is and ought to be totally dissolved; and that as Free and Independent States, they have full Power to levy War, conclude Peace, contract Alliances, establish Commerce, and to do all other Acts and Things which Independent States may of right do.

And for the support of this Declaration, with a firm reliance on the protection of divine Providence, we mutually pledge to each other our Lives, our Fortunes, and our Sacred Honor.

☆

by Thomas Jefferson

☆

Friends and Fellow Citizens: Called upon to undertake the duties of the first executive office of our country, I avail myself of the presence of that portion of my fellow citizens which is here assembled, to express my grateful thanks for the favor with which they have been pleased to look toward me, to declare a sincere consciousness that the task is above my talents, and that I approach it with those anxious and awful presentiments which the greatness of the charge and the weakness of my powers so justly inspire. A rising nation, spread over a wide and fruitful land, traversing all the seas with the rich productions of their industry, engaged in commerce with nations who feel power and forget right, advancing rapidly to destinies beyond the reach of mortal eye—when I contemplate these transcendent objects, and see the honor, the happiness, and the hopes of this beloved country committed to the issue and the auspices of this day, I shrink from the contemplation, and humble myself before the magnitude of the undertaking. Utterly indeed, should I despair, did not the presence of many whom I here see remind me, that in other high authorities provided by our Constitution, I shall find resources of wisdom, of virtue, and of zeal, on which to rely under all difficulties. To you, then, gentlemen, who are charged with the sovereign functions of legislation, and to those associated with you, I look with encouragement for that guidance and support which may enable us to steer with safety the vessel in which we are all embarked amid the conflicting elements of a troubled world.

During the contest of opinion through which we have passed, the animation of discussion and of exertions has sometimes worn an aspect which might impose on strangers unused to think freely and to speak and to write what they think; but this being now decided by the voice of the nation, announced according to the rules of the Constitution, all will, of course, arrange themselves under the will of the law, and unite in common efforts for the common good. All, too, will bear in mind this sacred principle, that though the will of the majority is in all cases to prevail, that will, to be rightful, must be reasonable; that the minority possess their equal rights, which equal laws must protect, and to violate which would be oppression. Let us, then, fellow citizens, unite with one heart and one mind. Let us restore to social intercourse that harmony and affection without which liberty and even life itself are but dreary things. And let us reflect that having banished from our land that religious intolerance under which mankind so long bled and suffered, we have yet gained little if we countenance a political intolerance as despotic, as wicked, and capable of as bitter and bloody persecutions. During the throes and convulsions of the ancient world, during the agonizing spasms of infuriated man, seeking through blood and slaughter his long-lost liberty, it was not wonderful that the agitations of the billows should reach even this distant and peaceful shore; that this should be more felt and feared by some and less by others; that this should divide opinions as to measures of safety. But every difference of opinion is not a difference of principle. We have called by different names brethren of the same principle. We are all republicans—we are all federalists.

If there be any among us who would wish to dissolve this Union or to change its republican form, let them stand undisturbed as monuments of the safety with which error of opinion may be tolerated where reason is left free to combat it. I know, indeed, that some honest men fear that a republican government cannot be strong; that this government is not strong enough. But would the honest patriot, in the full tide of successful experiment, abandon a government which has so far kept us free and firm, on the theoretic and visionary fear that this government, the world's best hope, may by possibility want energy to preserve itself? I trust not. I believe this, on the contrary, the strongest government on earth. I believe it is the only one where every man, at the call of the laws, would fly to the standard of the law, and would meet invasions of the public order as his own personal concern. Sometimes it is said that man cannot be trusted with the government of himself. Can he, then, be trusted with the government of others? Or have we found angels in the form of kings to govern him? Let history answer this question.

Let us, then, with courage and confidence pursue our own federal and republican principles, our attachment to our union and representative government. Kindly separated by nature and a wide ocean from the exterminating

havoc of one quarter of the globe; too high-minded to endure the degradations of the others; possessing a chosen
country, with room enough for entertaining a due sense
of our equal right to the use of our own faculties, to the
acquisitions of our industry, to honor and confidence from
our fellow citizens, resulting not from birth but from our
actions and their sense of them; enlightened by a benign
religion, professed, indeed, and practiced in various forms,
yet all of them including honesty, truth, temperance, gratitude, and the love of man; acknowledging and adoring
an overruling Providence, which by all its dispensations
proves that it delights in the happiness of man here and
his greater happiness hereafter; with all these blessings,
what more is necessary to make us a happy and prosperous
people? Still one thing more, fellow citizens—a wise and
frugal government, which shall restrain men from injur-
ing one another, which shall leave them otherwise free to
regulate their own pursuits of industry and improvement,
and shall not take from the mouth of labor the bread it has
earned. This is the sum of good government, and this is
necessary to close the circle of our felicities.

About to enter, fellow citizens, on the exercise of duties
which comprehend everything dear and valuable to you,
it is proper that you should understand what I deem the
essential principles of our government, and consequently
those which ought to shape its administration. I will com-
press them within the narrowest compass they will bear,
stating the general principle, but not all its limitations.
Equal and exact justice to all men, of whatever state or
persuasion, religious or political; peace, commerce, and

honest friendship, with all nations—entangling alliances with none; the support of the state governments in all their rights, as the most competent administrations for our domestic concerns and the surest bulwarks against antirepublican tendencies; the preservation of the general government in its whole constitutional vigor, as the sheet anchor of our peace at home and safety abroad; a jealous care of the right of election by the people—a mild and safe corrective of abuses which are lopped by the sword of the revolution where peaceable remedies are unprovided; absolute acquiescence in the decisions of the majority—the vital principle of republics, from which there is no appeal but to force, the vital principle and immediate parent of despotism; a well-disciplined militia—our best reliance in peace and for the first moments of war, till regulars may relieve them; the supremacy of the civil over the military authority; economy in the public expense, that labor may be lightly burdened; the honest payment of our debts and sacred preservation of the public faith; encouragement of agriculture, and of commerce as its handmaid; the diffusion of information and the arraignment of all abuses at the bar of public reason; freedom of religion; freedom of the press; freedom of person under the protection of the habeas corpus; and trial by juries impartially selected—these principles form the bright constellation which has gone before us, and guided our steps through an age of revolution and reformation. The wisdom of our sages and the blood of our heroes have been devoted to their attainment. They should be the creed of our political faith—the text of civil instruction—the touchstone by which to try the services of those we trust; and should we wander from them in moments of error or alarm, let us hasten to retrace our steps and to regain the road which alone leads to peace, liberty, and safety.

I repair, then, fellow citizens, to the post you have assigned me. With experience enough in subordinate offices to have seen the difficulties of this, the greatest of all, I have learned to expect that it will rarely fall to the lot of imperfect man to retire from this station with the reputation and the favor which bring him into it. Without pretensions to that high confidence reposed in our first and great Revolutionary character, whose preeminent services had entitled him to the first place in his country's love, and destined for him the fairest page in the volume of faithful history, I ask so much confidence only as may give firmness and effect to the legal administration of your affairs. I shall often go wrong through defect of judgment. When right, I shall often be thought wrong by those whose positions will not command a view of the whole ground. I ask your indulgence for my own errors, which will never be intentional; and your support against the errors of others, who may condemn what they would not if seen in all its parts. The approbation implied by your suffrage is a consolation to me for the past; and my future solicitude will be to retain the good opinion of those who have bestowed it in advance, to conciliate that of others by doing them all the good in my power, and to be instrumental to the happiness and freedom of all.

Relying, then, on the patronage of your good will, I advance with obedience to the work, ready to retire from it whenever you become sensible how much better choice it is in your power to make. And may that Infinite Power which rules the destinies of the universe, lead our councils to what is best, and give them a favorable issue for your peace and prosperity.

SEEDS OF DESTINY

☆

by Charles Evans Hughes
Chief Justice, United States Supreme Court, 1930-41

☆

You cannot be saved by valor and devotion to your ancestors. To each generation comes its patriotic duty, and upon your willingness to sacrifice and endure, as those before you have sacrificed and endured, rests the national hope.

From a speech, "What the Flag Means," given in 1916

FACES TO THE SUN

☆

by Inez Clark Thorson

1944

☆

Man's ancient heritage, freedom's light,
The forge on which his heart may shape a dream,
The blaze that warms, the bread that feeds the soul,
The word of wisdom teaching him the right
Of fellowmen to build what each may deem
A highway leading to a splendid goal.
In Freedom's Way men call each other friend—
The humble man may reach a high estate
Unhampered by the accident of birth.
And thus it follows that unto this end,
Since freedom does not make its bed with hate,
The blood of men has long profaned the earth.

The way of love is ever freedom's way—
The hand-clasp in the dark to still a fear,
A sorrow shared until the sting is done—
It is a jewel for which brave men pay
Their last, warm drop of blood that those most dear
To them may walk with faces to the sun!

☆

FOR A RENAISSANCE OF FAITH

☆

by Peter Marshall

☆

Our Father, remove from us the sophistication of our age and the skepticism that has come, like a frost, to blight our faith and to make it weak. Bring us back to a faith that makes men great and strong, a faith that enables us to love and to live, the faith by which we are triumphant, the faith by which alone we can walk with Thee. We pray for a return of that simple faith, that old-fashioned trust in God, that made strong and great the homes of our ancestors who built this good land and who in building left us our heritage.

In the strong name of Jesus, our Lord, we make this prayer. Amen.

HE LOOKED TOMORROW STRAIGHT IN THE EYE

☆

John Hancock Mutual Life Insurance Company, 1951

☆

Sometimes I wish that Tom Jefferson were here to talk things over. I think he'd know what is on my mind.

Tom lived in a time of trouble, just as we do. He knew war and the threat of war, and that unquiet sense of a nameless dread in the air. He knew what it means to go to bed at night never knowing if the things you care about will still be there in the morning.

And yet, if I read my book right, nobody ever saw Tom worried. Nobody saw him scared. Nobody saw Tom anything but cheerful about the way things were going to turn out.

I think of those uneasy years when Tom and other men of the Colonies were wrestling with an appalling decision: whether the people of this country were ready to stand on their own feet. We know now how right their answer was—but what made Tom so sure, back then?

I think of Tom as our first Secretary of State, easy and confident that this new little republic could hold its own in the world. How did he know, back then?

And I think of Tom in the White House, facing problems day and night that could mean disaster for a young country, and never doubting the outcome at all.

I think I know why Tom was sure.

Tom had a feeling about the people of this country.

He felt that God put good stuff in them, and that freedom brought it out. He never doubted for a minute that in the plain, everyday, self-respecting, unbossed men and women of America there would always be strength enough, and wisdom enough, and courage enough to handle anything fate might deal out.

And Tom meant me. And he meant you.

That's why, sometimes, I wish that Thomas Jefferson might come striding back today, with his big farmer's shoulders and those mild gray eyes of his—back to the America that was once just an idea in his head, and to the people he believed in though they hadn't yet been born.

I'd like Tom to see that he wasn't wrong.

☆

I BELIEVE

☆

by Senator Robert A. Taft (1889-1954)

From A Foreign Policy for Americans, *1951*

☆

[I believe that] we should battle the principles of communism and socialism and convince the world that its true happiness lies in the establishment of a system of liberty; that communism and socialism are the very antithesis of liberalism, and that only a nation conceived in liberty can hope to bring real happiness to its people or the world.

☆

GOD SAVE THE FLAG

☆

by Oliver Wendell Holmes (1809-94)

☆

Washed in the blood of the brave and the blooming,
Snatched from the altars of insolent foes,
Burning with star-fires, but never consuming,
Flash its broad ribbons of lily and rose.

Vainly the prophets of Baal would rend it,
Vainly his worshippers pray for its fall;
Thousands have died for it, millions defend it,
Emblem of justice and mercy to all:

Justice that reddens the sky with her terrors,
Mercy that comes with her white-handed train,
Soothing all passions, redeeming all errors,
Sheathing the sabre and breaking the chain.

Borne on the deluge of old usurpations,
Drifted our Ark o'er the desolate seas,
Bearing the rainbow of hope to the nations,
Torn from the storm-cloud and flung to the breeze!

God Bless the Flag and its loyal defenders,
While its broad folds o'er the battlefield wave,
Till the dim star-wreath rekindle its splendors,
Washed from its stains in the blood of the brave!

MY PEOPLE CAME TO THIS COUNTRY

☆

by *Struthers Burt*

1942

☆

My people came to this country
In need of a land that was free,
So I think the only thing I can do,
If a decent man I would be,
Is to walk with my head held high and **proud**
For the blood that runs in me.

My people came to this country
—And the seas were a green great space—
Because the trees were kind and tall
And the fields a pleasant place,
And brave men worshipped as they **would**
And thought with an open face.

Beat in memory ancient drums
Like the throbbing of a vein;
Wave on the winds of a continent
Ragged flags in the rain,
For the ghosts of countless countrymen
Are on the march again.

My people came to this country
With dreams too quick for hate;
A neighbor was a light in the dark

☆

Or a hand upon a gate,
And whence he came was no news at all
In the building of a state.

Now God bless every stick of it
And every path and post;
The broad slow rivers of the south,
The quick bright streams of the frost,
And the mountains like a mighty oath
That does not count the cost.

And God bless all the dipping fields
From the mountains to the sea,
And grant that I walk like a fearless man
For the blood that runs in me.

WHEN THE NAVY WENT TO MOLOKAI

☆

by Henry F. Unger

1950

☆

President Theodore Roosevelt read the letter from far-off Molokai Leper Colony. It was simply signed Joseph Dutton. For a few minutes the President remained in deep thought. Then he put through a phone call to Secretary of the Navy Newberry.

Minutes later, Rear Admiral C. S. Sperry, standing on the bridge of the flagship *Connecticut* in Honolulu harbor, got an urgent wireless dispatch. "Divert from course —Pass Molokai Island in battle formation—Show naval power to Brother Dutton—Dip color—Then continue Japan. . . . ."

It was the morning of July 16, 1908. On gray, lofty Molokai, once the dread site for abandoned lepers, sixty-five-year-old Dutton moved briskly about his humble home. He was manager of the leper colony now, successor to heroic Father Damien, who had died from the disease in 1889.

Flag-raising each morning was his prime joy. Tenderly he held the folded flag, preparatory to moving outdoors to the flagpole on a promontory overlooking the Pacific.

Suddenly a young leper threw open the screen door. "Brother Dutton—many ships—far off!"

"Ships, ships?"

As the impact of the words hit him, the old man

grasped the flag tightly and strode out into the warm morning.

A small group, attracted by the boy's cries, babbled excitedly outside the house. The U.S. Navy was coming— the big American ships about which Brother Dutton had so often boasted to his lepers. But they would pass only on the horizon—Dutton was sure of that. His weak, tired eyes would barely catch the fleet's outline.

The gray-haired samaritan of Molokai walked swiftly toward the promontory. "There!" the boy shouted. Brother Dutton uttered a chuckle as he noted the bow of a ship pointed toward Molokai.

"The Navy is coming!" he cried. "Quick, let's put up the flag!"

Dutton's hands trembled. For years he had told the lepers of the paradise that was America. They gaped as he told of the nation's great naval power. Now it was on the horizon and heading toward their isolated island.

Holding the line with one gnarled hand, Dutton slowly pulled the flag skyward. His lepers, grouped around the pole, stood at attention. For twenty-two years, Dutton had raised and lowered this flag each day.

As the big battleships drew closer to the island, whooping lepers were quieted by Dutton. "We must stand at attention as the ships pass, out of respect to the Government."

Dutton and his lepers tensed as the four battle divisions moved closer. Thoughts rushed through Dutton's mind as the first division—the *Vermont, Kansas, Connecticut,* and *Louisiana*—churned into view.

He was a discharged Union soldier, printer, drugstore clerk, his mother a schoolmarm, his father a shoemaker in Stowe, Vermont . . . Now came the turrets of the second division, the *Georgia, New Jersey, Rhode Island*, and *Virginia* . . . Once he had been a member of the severe Trappist Monastery in Kentucky . . . Now the third division, the *Maine, Minnesota, Ohio,* and *Missouri,* swept into position.

Over Dutton's head, puffs of Hawaiian breeze curled the flag . . . Now came the final division, the *Alabama, Kentucky, Illinois,* and *Kearsage.* The armed sea power of a great nation was parading before the Union veteran's gaze.

The samaritan of Molokai couldn't believe his eyes. It was so different in 1886, when he disembarked here from a packet ship. A story in a New Orleans newspaper had told about Father Damien's work among the lepers, and Joseph Dutton quickly bought a one-way ticket to Molokai, never again to see America.

Now the fleet was maneuvering into battle formation. Slowly, the flagship passed the promontory. Suddenly the colors were dipped and the crews saluted. Misty-eyed Dutton, frail but standing like a ramrod, returned the salute as the entire fleet passed, each ship dipping her colors.

As the lepers watched the receding ships, tears rolled down their ravaged faces. Brother Dutton, who had corresponded with the world's great from his lonely leper island, had brought the Fleet to them, the forgotten outcasts of Molokai.

☆

AMERICA

☆

by Samuel Francis Smith (*1808-95*)

☆

My country, 'tis of thee,
Sweet Land of Liberty,
    Of thee I sing;
Land where my fathers died,
Land of the pilgrims' pride,
From every mountainside
    Let Freedom ring.

My native country, thee,
Land of the noble free,
    Thy name I love;
I love thy rocks and rills,
Thy woods and templed hills,
My heart with rapture thrills
    Like that above.

Let music swell the breeze
And ring from all the trees,
    Sweet Freedom's song;
Let mortal tongues awake;
Let all that breathe partake;
Let rocks their silence break,
    The sound prolong.

Our fathers' God, to Thee,
Author of Liberty,
  To Thee we sing;
Long may our land be bright
With Freedom's Holy light;
Protect us by Thy might,
  Great God, our King.

☆

TYPICAL AMERICAN

☆

by Nicholas Murray Butler (*1862-1947*)
American educator

☆

The typical American is he who, whether rich or poor, whether dwelling in the North, South, East or West, whether scholar, professional man, merchant, manufacturer, farmer, or skilled worker for wages, lives the life of a good citizen and a good neighbor; who believes loyally and with all his heart in his country's institutions, and in the underlying principles on which these institutions are built; who directs both his private and his public life by sound principles; who cherishes high ideals; and who aims to train his children for a useful life and for their country's service.

From The American as He Is, *1908*

PLEDGE OF ALLEGIANCE

☆

I pledge allegiance to the Flag of the United States of America and to the Republic for which it stands, one nation under God, indivisible, with liberty and justice for all.

☆

GOD BLESS THE RED AND THE GRAY

☆

Robert Gordon Smith

☆

For something like two centuries the Red Man battled against growing odds to turn back from this magnificent land the onward sweep of the Palefaces who came over the sea; and for four bloody, tragic years the Boys in Gray fought gloriously in a losing cause.

This is not the book in which to judge the rights and the wrongs of those epic struggles that have played so great a part in the Story of America, but this much I know: The Indians who roamed these forests and plains and mountains, and the men and women who served under the Stars and Bars have left rich legacies in the very life of our country that grow more precious through the years.

Whatever their faults and errors—and we must all come humbly to the Throne of God's Grace seeking forgiveness for our own—they gave their best for those things in which they truly believed, and in their ways of life and codes of honor there were virtues and ideals that have become an everlasting part of the America we love.

God Bless the Red and the Gray.

HIAWATHA'S DEPARTURE

☆

by Henry Wadsworth Longfellow
from Hiawatha, *1855*

☆

By the shore of Gitche Gumee,
By the shining Big-Sea-Water,
At the doorway of his wigwam,
In the pleasant Summer morning,
Hiawatha stood and waited.
All the air was full of freshness,
All the earth was bright and joyous,
And before him, through the sunshine,
Westward toward the neighboring forest
Passed in golden swarms the Ahmo,
Passed the bees, the honey-makers,
Burning, singing in the sunshine.

Bright before him shone the heavens,
Level spread the lake before him;
From its bosom leaped the sturgeon,
Sparkling, flashing in the sunshine;
On its margin the great forest
Stood reflected in the water,
Every tree-top had its shadow,
Motionless beneath the water.

From the brow of Hiawatha
Gone was every trace of sorrow,
As the fog spread off the water,
As the mist from off the meadow.
With a smile of joy and triumph,
With a look of exultation,
As of one who in a vision
Sees what is to be, but is not,
Stood and waited Hiawatha.

Toward the sun his hands were lifted,
Both the palms spread out against it,
And between the parted fingers
Fell the sunshine on his features,
Flecked with light his naked shoulders,
As it falls and flecks an oak tree
Through the rifted leaves and branches.

O'er the water floating, flying,
Something in the hazy distance,
Something in the mists of morning,
Loomed and lifted from the water,
Now seemed floating, now seemed flying,
Coming nearer, nearer, nearer.

Was it Shingebis the diver?
Or the pelican, the Shada?
Or the heron, the Shuh-shuh-gah?
Or the white goose, Waw-be-wawa,

With the water dripping, flashing,
From its glossy neck and feathers?

It was neither goose nor diver,
Neither pelican nor heron,
O'er the water floating, flying,
Through the shining mist of morning,
But a birch canoe with paddles,
Rising, sinking on the water,
Dripping, flashing in the sunshine;
And within it came a people
From the distant land of Wabun,
From the farthest realms of morning
Came the Black-Robe chief, the Prophet,
He the Priest of Prayer, the Paleface,
With his guides and his companions.

And the noble Hiawatha,
With his hands aloft extended,
Held aloft in sign of welcome,
Waited, full of exultation,
Till the birch canoe with paddles
Grated on the shining pebbles,
Stranded on the sandy margin,
Till the Black-Robe chief, the Paleface,
With the cross upon his bosom,
Landed on the sandy margin.

Then the joyous Hiawatha
Cried aloud and spake in this wise:

"Beautiful is the sun, O strangers,
When you come so far to see us!
All our town in peace awaits you,
All our doors stand open for you;
You shall enter all our wigwams,
For the heart's right hand we give you."

· · · · · · · · · · · · · ·

And the Black-Robe chief made answer,
Stammered in his speech a little,
Speaking words yet unfamiliar:
"Peace be with you, Hiawatha,
Peace be with you and your people,
Peace of prayer, and peace of pardon,
Peace of Christ, and joy of Mary!"

· · · · · · · · · · · · , ·

Then the Black-Robe chief, the Prophet,
Told his message to the people,
Told the purport of his mission,
Told them of the Virgin Mary,
And her blessed Son, the Saviour,
How in distant lands and ages
He had lived on earth as we do;
How he fasted, prayed, and labored;
How he rose from where they laid him,
Walked again with his disciples,
And ascended into heaven.

And the chiefs made answer, saying:
"We have listened to your message,
We have heard your words of wisdom,

We will think on what you tell us.
It is well for us, O brothers,
That you come so far to see us!"

. . . .

Slowly o'er the simmering landscape
Fell the evening's dusk and coolness,
And the long and level sunbeams
Shot their spears into the forest,
Breaking through its shields of shadow,
Rushed into each secret ambush,
Searched each thicket, dingle, hollow;
Still the guests of Hiawatha
Slumbered in the silent wigwam.

From his place rose Hiawatha,
Bade farewell to old Nokomis,
Spake in whispers, spake in this wise,
    "I am going, O Nokomis,
On a long and distant journey,
To the portals of the Sunset,
To the regions of the home-wind,
Of the Northwest Wind, Keewaydin.
But these guests I leave behind me,
In your watch and ward I leave them;
See that never harm comes near them,
See that never fear molests them,
Never danger nor suspicion,
Never want of food or shelter,
In the lodge of Hiawatha!"

Forth into the village went he,
Bade farewell to all the warriors,
Bade farewell to all the young men,
Spake persuading, spake in this wise:
"I am going, O my people,
On a long and distant journey;
Many moons and many winters
Will have come, and will have vanished,
Ere I come again to see you.
But my guests I leave behind me;
Listen to their words of wisdom,
Listen to the truth they tell you,
For the Master of Life has sent them
From the land of light and morning!"

On the shore stood Hiawatha,
Turned and waved his hand at parting;
On the clear and luminous water
Launched his birch canoe for sailing,
From the pebbles of the margin
Shoved it forth into the water;
Whispered to it, "Westward! westward!"
And with speed it darted forward.

And the evening sun descending
Set the clouds on fire with redness,
Burned the broad sky, like a prairie,
Left upon the level water
One long track and trail of splendor,

Down whose stream, as down a river,
Westward, westward Hiawatha
Sailed into the fiery sunset,
Sailed into the purple vapors,
Sailed into the dusk of evening.

And the people from the margin
Watched him floating, rising, sinking,
Till the birch canoe seemed lifted
High into that sea of splendor,
Till it sank into the vapors
Like the new moon slowly, slowly
Sinking in the purple distance.

And they said, "Farewell forever!"
Said, "Farewell, O Hiawatha!"
And the forests, dark and lonely,
Moved through all their depths of darkness,
Sighed, "Farewell, O Hiawatha!"
And the waves upon the margin
Rising, rippling on the pebbles,
Sobbed, "Farewell, O Hiawatha!"
And the heron, the Shuh-shuh-gah,
From her haunts among the fen-lands,
Screamed, "Farewell, O Hiawatha!"

Thus departed Hiawatha,
Hiawatha the Beloved,
In the glory of the sunset,
In the purple mists of evening,

To the regions of the home-wind,
Of the Northwest Wind, Keewaydin,
To the Islands of the Blessed,
To the Kingdom of Ponemah,
To the Land of the Hereafter!

☆

A SONG OF AMERICA

☆

by Walt Whitman

From A Carol of Harvest, *1867*

☆

Ever upon this stage,
Is acted God's calm, annual drama,
Gorgeous processions, songs of birds,
Sunrise, that fullest feeds and freshens most the soul,
The heaving sea, the waves upon the shore, the musical,
   strong waves,
The woods, the stalwart trees, the slender, tapering trees,
The flowers, the grass, the lilliput, countless armies of the
   grass,
The heat, the showers, the measureless pasturages,
The scenery of the snows, the winds' free orchestra,
The stretching, light-hung roof of clouds—the clear ceru-
   lean, and the bulging, silvery fringes,
The high dilating stars, the placid, beckoning stars,
The moving flocks and herds, the plains and emerald
   meadows,
The shows of all the varied lands, and all the growths and
   products.

Fecund America! Today,
Thou art all over set in births and joys!
Thou groan'st with riches! thy wealth clothes thee as with
   a swathing garment!

Thou laughest loud with ache of great possessions!

A myriad-twining life, like interlacing vines, binds all thy vast demesne!

As some huge ship, freighted to water's edge, thou ridest into port!

As rain falls from the heaven, and vapors rise from earth, so have the precious values fallen upon thee, and risen out of thee!

Thou envy of the globe! thou miracle!

Thou, bathed, choked, swimming in plenty!

Thou lucky Mistress of the tranquil barns!

Thou Prairie Dame that sittest in the middle, and lookest out upon thy world, and lookest East, and lookest West!

Dispensatress, that by a word givest a thousand miles— that giv'st a million farms, and missest nothing!

Thou All-Acceptress—thou Hospitable—(thou only art hospitable, as God is hospitable.)

. . . .

I see where America, Mother of All,

Well pleased, with full-spanning eye, gazes forth, dwells long,

And counts the varied gathering of the products.

Busy the far, the sunlit panorama;

Prairie, orchard, and yellow grain of the North,

Cotton and rice of the South, and Louisianian cane;

Open, unseeded fallows, rich fields of clover and timothy,

Kine and horses feeding, and droves of sheep and swine,

And many a stately river flowing, and many a jocund brook,

And healthy uplands with their herby-perfumed breezes,

And the good green grass—that delicate miracle, the ever
    recurring grass.

. . . .

Well pleased, America, thou beholdest,
Over the fields of the West, those crawling monsters,
The human-divine inventions, the labor-saving imple-
    ments:
Beholdest, moving in every direction, imbued as with life,
    the revolving hay-rakes,
The steam-power reaping machines, and the horsepower
    machines,
The engines, thrashers of grain, and cleaners of grain,
    well separating the straw—the nimble work of the pat-
    ent pitchfork;
Beholdest the newer sawmill, the southern cotton gin, and
    the rice-cleaner.

Beneath thy look, O Maternal,
With these, and else, and with their own strong hands,
    the Heroes harvest.
All gather, and all harvest;
(Yet but for thee, O Powerful! not a scythe might swing,
    as now, in security;
Not a maize stalk dangle, as now, its silken tassels in
    peace.)

Under Thee only they harvest—even but a wisp of hay,
    under thy great face, only;
Harvest the maize of Missouri, Kentucky, Tennessee—each
    ear in its light-green sheath,

Harvest the wheat of Ohio, Illinois, Wisconsin—every
barbed spear, under thee;
Gather the hay to its myriad mows, in the odorous, tran-
quil barns,
Oats to their bins—the white potato, the buckwheat of
Michigan, to theirs;
Gather the cotton in Mississippi or Alabama, dig and
hoard the golden, the sweet potato of Georgia and the
Carolinas,
Clip the wool of California or Pennsylvania,
Cut the flax in the Middle States, or hemp, or tobacco in
the Borders,
Pick the pea and the bean, or pull apples from the trees,
or bunches of grapes from the vines,
Or aught that ripens in all these States, or North or South,
Under the beaming sun, and under Thee.

MAY WE ALWAYS REMEMBER

☆

by Andrew Jackson

From Farewell Address, March 4, 1837

☆

You have the highest of human trusts committed to your care. Providence has showered on this favored land blessings without number and has chosen you as the guardians of freedom, to preserve it for the benefit of the human race. May He who holds in His hands the destinies of nations make you worthy of the favors He has bestowed and enable you, with pure hearts and pure hands and sleepless vigilance, to guard and defend to the end of time the charge He has committed to your keeping.

THE STRENGTH OF AMERICAN DEMOCRACY

☆

by *James Bryce* (*1838-1922*)

British diplomat, legislator, and writer
From The American Commonwealth, *1888*

☆

Democracy has not only taught the Americans how to use liberty without abusing it, and how to secure equality: it has also taught them fraternity. . . . . . There is still in the United States a sort of kindliness, a sense of human fellowship, a recognition of the duty of mutual help owed by man to man, stronger than anywhere in the Old World, and certainly stronger than in the upper or middle classes of England, France, or Germany. The natural impulse of every citizen in America is to respect every citizen, and to feel that citizenship constitutes a certain ground of respect. The idea of each man's equal rights is so fully realized that the rich or powerful man feels it is no indignity to take his turn among the crowd, and does not expect any deference from the poorest. . . . . .

Wealth is generally felt to be a trust. . . . . . No one, for instance, thinks of shutting up his pleasure-grounds; he seldom even builds a wall round them, but puts up only a low railing, so that the sight of his trees and shrubs is enjoyed by passers-by. That anyone should be permitted by opinion or by law to seal up many square miles of beautiful mountain country against tourists or artists is to the ordinary American almost incredible. Such things are to him the marks of a land still groaning under feudal tyranny.

THE PROMISE OF AMERICA

☆

by Thomas Wolfe (*1900-38*)
From You Can't Go Home Again, *1940*

☆

To every man his chance—
to every man,
regardless of his birth, his
shining golden opportunity—
to every man the right
to live, to work, to be himself,
and to become whatever thing
his manhood and his vision
can combine to make him—
this, seeker, is
the promise of America.

☆

WHAT AMERICA MEANS TO ME

☆

by Charles C. Spaulding (*1874-1952*)

1948

☆

The other day I read a newspaper item in which a man in Moscow said it was a mockery to call America a land of opportunity. America's opportunities, he said, were limited to the privileged few.

My background was probably as humble as backgrounds can be. Yet I found many opportunities for enterprise and no man tried to stand in my way. When I paid the price in heartaches that any enterpriser pays, America lavished rewards upon me.

I preside over a life insurance company that has 131 million dollars' worth of insurance in force, and a bank that has five million dollars in resources. I am a director of a bonding company, a building and loan association, and a fire insurance company. I am trustee of Howard University, Shaw University, and North Carolina College at Durham; chairman of the board of a large hospital; and I have been invited to conferences at the White House.

I was born one of fourteen children on a small cotton farm in North Carolina ten years after the Emancipation. My father, Benjamin Spaulding, believed in the Promise of America. He never became disillusioned by the realities of freedom as thousands of colored people did; he never expected something for nothing. He realized that the Promise had to be redeemed by years of sweat, thrift and enterprise.

My father refused to hate any man. He practiced neigh-borly cooperation with everybody. He lived to own a prosperous farm, and to be a leader in his community. His success story is vastly more impressive than mine, because —starting with Emancipation—he had to work out a com-pletely new pattern of existence.

Too many people, I believe, think America is a land of gushing riches, and are disgruntled if they don't get their share. America is no such place. It is a land of challenges.

The pioneering spirit still profoundly shapes American beliefs and attitudes. Americans warmheartedly applaud any man, whatever his origin or color, who breaks new ground or attains new heights, whether he be Henry Ford or Joe Louis.

The great satisfaction in my life is that I have spent most of my days pioneering. I left the farm at twenty, to com-plete an eighth-grade education. So, a grown man among children, I studied spelling and arithmetic—and washed dishes at $10 a month at a Durham, North Carolina hotel to earn my way.

Soon after my graduation, two men of my race, John Merrick and A. M. Moore, offered me the job of general manager of the insurance company they were trying to de-velop. I was also to be sole agent, clerk, and janitor. My pay was to come out of my commissions.

Merrick and Moore formed the company mainly to end a humiliating practice which our people had to resort to at funerals: passing the hat "so that we can bury this brother." A policyholder, by paying us, say, twenty cents a week,

could be assured of getting $4 a week if he became sick, or
his beneficiary would get a lump sum if he died. But most
of my people were suspicious and I met considerable sales
resistance.

Then one day came the crisis which almost finished us—
and proved to be a major turning point. The very first man
I insured died six weeks after I signed him up. When his
widow rushed in a claim for $40 death benefits, I promised
to take care of it "right away." Of the money collected
from policyholders in six weeks, I now had only twenty-
nine cents. The rest had gone for operating expenses. I
called an emergency meeting with my two senior executives. They dug into their private funds, and the widow
was paid at once.

The episode showed me my profound ignorance of life
insurance. I had never even heard of mortality tables. I began consulting the Durham representative of the Metro-
politan Life Insurance Company. He patiently taught me
how to calculate the life expectancy of a prospect.

Gradually our business gained momentum. Sometimes
our worst obstacles turned out to be opportunities in dis-
guise. When no company would bond our agents, we
solved the problem by forming our own bonding company.

This gave us other ideas. There were no fire insurance
companies willing to insure personal property owned by
our people, few banks really interested in helping them buy
homes. We entered these fields by setting up our own cor-
porations, and are still operating them—forty-nine years
later.

As our enterprises increased in prestige, persons of all backgrounds matter-of-factly began dealing with us. We have some white insurance policyholders, and any day that you walk into our Mechanics & Farmers Bank you will see several white merchants conferring with our officers about their problems.

I will never forget the help some white men gave us when we were struggling to launch our insurance company. In our earliest, darkest days, Washington Duke, the famed tobacco tycoon; Judge R. W. Winston, the noted Carolina jurist; and his partner, V. S. Bryant, Sr., spent many hours giving us shrewd advice. When we started our bank, every afternoon for several weeks the white president of the Citizens National Bank came in to help us straighten our books. In 1933, during the banking crisis, the State Banking Commissioner called several of Durham's leading bankers and said, "Spaulding says he wants to open Monday morning. But what if they stage a real knockout run on him?" Without exception, the bankers replied, "Tell Spaulding that as long as we have money, he will have it."

There has been a great deal of just criticism made about the South. While it may be America's Number One Problem, I think it is America's Number One Opportunity for men of good will, prudence, and character. The great news in the South today is that an increasing number of men of both races are working together amicably for the greater prosperity and well-being of all.

Throughout America my people are maturing and prospering—and launching their own enterprises. During the past decade the number of my people who became managers, skilled craftsmen, and business executives has more than doubled.

Negroes have been achieving success in various fields of endeavor: Paul Williams, of Los Angeles, is regarded as one of America's leading architects; Dr. Charles Drew, who perfected the blood-plasma bank, is a world-famous scientist; William Hastie, Governor of the Virgin Islands, is a respected administrator; A. A. Austin, of New York, buys and sells skyscrapers; Dr. Ralph J. Bunche, who succeeded Count Folke Bernadotte as United Nations mediator in Palestine, is an outstanding diplomat.

Many business leaders are emerging in the South. In Atlanta, two Negroes operate a chain of fine drugstores, and I can take you to several spacious plantations in the Old South that are owned by people of my race whose parents or grandparents worked there as slaves. A few months ago I visited the farm of David Jackson, of Adel, Georgia, who harvests $100,000 worth of produce each year and also does a big business renting his threshing machines to white and Negro farmers. Last year the people of my race had a total income of ten billion dollars—which, I will wager, would rival the entire income of the people of any one of several countries in Europe today.

I have traveled through fifteen European countries and am convinced that there is no place on this globe today where people, whatever their background, can make such progress as right here in America, provided they demonstrate ability, character and imagination.

I am seventy-four, but if I were a young man starting out today I would be excited about the opportunities now opening up in America. Because of our country's expanding prosperity and its constant technological advances, opportunities today are far greater than they were fifty years ago.

America depends for its growth upon bold young men willing to take a chance in pioneering new fields of service. And it bountifully rewards the skillful pioneer, whatever his origin.

THE NEW COLOSSUS

☆

by *Emma Lazarus* (*1849-87*)

☆

Not like the brazen giant of Greek fame,
With conquering limbs astride from land to land;
Here at our sea-washed, sunset gates shall stand
A mighty woman with a torch, whose flame
Is the imprisoned lightning, and her name
Mother of Exiles. From her beacon hand
Glows world-wide welcome; her mild eyes command
The air-bridged harbor that twin cities frame.

"Keep, ancient lands, your storied pomp!" cries she
With silent lips. "Give me your tired, your poor,
Your huddled masses yearning to breathe free,
The wretched refuse of your teeming shore.
Send these, the homeless, tempest-tossed to me,
I lift my lamp beside the golden door."

LIGHTS FOR THE WORLD'S FIRST LADY

☆

Cities Service Company, July, 1951

☆

Once upon a time the famous Lady who stands in New York harbor was a Lady in the dark. Two men of Cities Service passed her one night on the Staten Island ferry.

"She ought to be lighted up," said George Williams.

"You're right," said Henry L. Doherty.

So, in the American tradition, they did something about it.

They enlisted the support of Joseph Pulitzer of the *New York World*, who carried on a campaign to interest school children in the Statue—and what it stands for—by getting them to contribute nickels and dimes to provide lights for the World's First Lady.

In addition to raising the money, there were many technical difficulties. Floodlighting was in its infancy. Another Cities Service man, Bob Carbutt, marshalled the skills of the nation's top engineers.

So it came to pass that on December 2, 1916, the World's First Lady came into her own. President Wilson gave the signal that transformed a "night-shrouded bulk to a glorious goddess, permanently blazing freedom's message." Following a parade from the Battery to the Waldorf, streets brilliantly lighted and lined with people, Wilson spoke at a banquet in honor of the occasion, and the thousand guests cheered a congratulatory message from the President of France.

The men and women of Cities Service are proud of the civic activities of its founders. For they are full-time citizens themselves, active in Red Cross and Community Chest campaigns, on the boards of Chambers of Commerce, schools, and hospitals. Right now they are working closely with the Government on the gas and petroleum problems of the Defense Program.

All this in the spirit of voluntary effort—the way of life symbolized by the Statue of Liberty.

AMERICA'S FAITH

☆

by Harry S. Truman

From Inaugural Address, January 20, 1949

☆

. . . . . The peoples of the earth face the future with grave uncertainty, composed almost equally of great hopes and great fears. In this time of doubt, they look to the United States as never before for good-will, strength, and wise leadership.

It is fitting, therefore, that we take this occasion to proclaim to the world the essential principles of the faith by which we live, and to declare our aims to all peoples.

The American people stand firm in the faith which has inspired this nation from the beginning. We believe that all men have a right to equal justice under law and equal opportunity to share in the common good. We believe that all men have the right to freedom of thought and expression. We believe that all men are created equal because they are created in the image of God.

From this faith we will not be moved.

The American people desire, and are determined to work for, a world in which all nations and all peoples are free to govern themselves as they see fit and to achieve a decent satisfying life.

. . . .

Events have brought our American democracy to new

☆

influence and new responsibilities. They will test our courage, our devotion to duty, and our concept of liberty.

But I say to all men: what we have achieved in liberty, we will surpass in greater liberty.

Steadfast in our faith in the Almighty, we will advance toward a world where man's freedom is secure.

To that end we will devote our strength, our resources, and our firmness of resolve. With God's help, the future of mankind will be assured in a world of justice, harmony, and peace.

I HEAR AMERICA SINGING

☆

by Walt Whitman

1860

☆

I hear America singing, the varied carols I hear;

Those of mechanics—each one singing his, as it should be, blithe and strong;

The carpenter singing his, as he measures his plank or beam,

The mason singing his, as he makes ready for work, or leaves off work;

The boatman singing what belongs to him in his boat—the deck-hand singing on the steamboat deck;

The shoemaker singing as he sits on his bench—the hatter singing as he stands;

The wood-cutter's song—the ploughboy's, on his way in the morning, or at the noon intermission, or at sundown;

The delicious singing of the mother—or of the young wife at work—or of the girl sewing or washing;

Each singing what belongs to him or her, and to none else;

The day what belongs to the day—at night, the party of young fellows, robust, friendly,

Singing with open mouths, their strong melodious songs.

☆

THE HOMES OF THE PEOPLE

☆

by Henry W. Grady (1850-89)

American journalist, editor, and orator

From "The Farmer and the Cities," a speech at
Elberton, Georgia, June, 1889

☆

A few Sundays ago I stood on a hill in Washington. My heart thrilled as I looked on the towering marble of my country's Capitol, and a mist gathered in my eyes as, standing there, I thought of its tremendous significance and the powers there assembled, and the responsibilities there centered. It seemed to me the best and mightiest sight that the sun could find in its wheeling course—this majestic home of a Republic that has taught the world its best lessons of liberty—and I felt that if wisdom and justice and honor abided therein, the world would stand indebted to this temple on which my eyes rested, and in which the ark of my covenant was lodged for its final uplifting and regeneration.

A few days later I visited a country home. A modest, quiet house sheltered by great trees and set in a circle of field and meadow, gracious with the promise of harvest; barns and cribs well filled and the old smokehouse odorous with treasure; the fragrance of pink and hollyhock mingling with the aroma of garden and orchard, and resonant with the hum of bees and poultry's busy clucking; inside the house, thrift, comfort, and that cleanliness that is next to godliness.

Outside stood the master, strong and wholesome and upright; wearing no man's collar; with no mortgage on his roof, and no lien on his ripening harvest; pitching his crops in his own wisdom, and selling them in his own time in his chosen market; master of his lands and master of himself.

Near by stood his aged father, happy in the heart and home of his son. And as they started to the house the old man's hand rested on the young man's shoulder, touching it with the knighthood of the fifth commandment, and laying there the unspeakable blessing of an honored and grateful father. As they drew near the door, the old mother appeared; the sunset falling on her face, softening its wrinkles and its tenderness, lighting up her patient eyes, and the rich music of her heart trembling on her lips, as in simple phrase she welcomed her husband and son to their home.

Beyond was the good wife, true of touch and tender, happy amid her household cares, clean of heart and conscience, the helpmate and the buckler of her husband. And the children, strong and sturdy, trooping down the lane with the lowing herd, or weary of simple sport, seeking, as truant birds do, the quiet of the old home nest. And I saw the night descend on that home, falling gently as from the wings of the unseen dove. And the stars swarmed in the bending skies, the trees thrilled with the cricket's cry, the restless bird called from the neighboring wood, and the father, a simple man of God, gathering the family about him, read from the Bible the old, old story of love and faith, and then went down in prayer, the baby hidden amid the folds of its mother's dress, and closed the record of that simple

☆

day by calling down the benediction of God on the family and the home!

And as I gazed, the memory of the great Capitol faded from my brain. Forgotten its treasure and its splendor. And I said, "Surely here—here in the homes of the people is lodged the ark of the covenant of my country. Here is its majesty and its strength. Here the beginning of its power and the end of its responsibility." The homes of the people; let us keep them pure and independent, and all will be well with the Republic.

The home is the source of our national life. Back of the national Capitol and above it stands the home. Back of the President and above him stands the citizen. What the home is, this and nothing else will the Capitol be. What the citizen wills, this and nothing else will the President be.

WHAT MAKES A NATION GREAT?

☆

by Alexander Blackburn (1844-1921)

☆

Not serried ranks with flags unfurled,
Not armored ships that gird the world,
Not hoarded wealth nor busy mills,
Not cattle on a thousand hills,
Not sages wise, nor schools nor laws,
Not boasted deeds in freedom's cause—
All these may be, and yet the state
In the eye of God be far from great.

That land is great which knows the Lord,
Whose songs are guided by His word;
Where justice rules twixt man and man,
Where love controls in art and plan;
Where, breathing in his native air,
Each soul finds joy in praise and prayer—
Thus may our country, good and great,
Be God's delight—man's best estate.

☆

MOTION FOR PRAYERS IN THE
CONSTITUTIONAL CONVENTION

☆

by Benjamin Franklin

June 28, 1787

☆

. . . . . I have lived, Sir, a long time; and the longer I live
the more convincing proofs I see of this truth, that God
governs in the Affairs of Men. And if a sparrow cannot
fall to the ground without His notice, is it probable that an
empire can rise without His aid?

We have been assured, Sir, in the Sacred Writings, that
"except the Lord build the House, they labor in vain that
build it." I firmly believe this; I also believe that, without
His concurring aid, we shall succeed in this political building no better than the Builders of Babel; we shall be divided by our little, partial, local interests, our projects will
be confounded, and we ourselves shall become a reproach
and a byword down to future ages. And what is worse,
Mankind may hereafter, from this unfortunate instance,
despair of establishing Government by human wisdom,
and leave it to chance, war, and conquest.

I therefore beg leave to move that henceforth Prayers,
imploring the Assistance of Heaven and Its Blessing on
our deliberations, be held in this Assembly every morning
before we proceed to business; and that one or more of
the clergy of this City be requested to officiate in that
service.

SOME OBSERVATIONS ON CURRENT AMERICAN LIFE

☆

by Herbert Hoover

From an address, February 13, 1960

☆

This republic is now 184 years old. It is older than any other great representative government in history. We have gone through seven wars, with series of crises before and after each one. We have gone through three great inflations with crises before and after. We have gone through the inevitable depressions from these inflations with accompanying crises. We have gone through a dozen crises of corruption in government.

Yet today we still possess most of the Bill of Rights, as handed down by the Founding Fathers 169 years ago. We are well fed, well clothed, fairly well housed; and we have the right to kick about any crisis.

This American way of life has proved to be pretty tough. But it needs to be even tougher right now.

I have lived a long life, and I have seen our nation rally, exert its strengths to surmount dangers as great as those which beset us today.

Among the signs of our moral and spiritual strength, I have witnessed the outpouring of compassion which saved the world from two gigantic famines that followed the two great wars. During forty-five years we provided the necessary margins of food, medical care, and clothing to 1,400,000,000 human beings who would otherwise have perished. And included among them were millions of people in our implacable enemy, Communist Russia.

And in these efforts we have restored healthy minds and bodies to over 16,000,000 children, who would have died from famine and disease, or would have become a danger to the world with their degenerate minds and dwarfed bodies.

Within my span of years, I have seen our voluntary organizations and institutions—devoted to religious service, charity, education, and community welfare—increase by tens of thousands in numbers and by billions of dollars in support.

I have witnessed elementary education expand to include practically all our children. Whatever complaints may be made about the system, it has practically abolished illiteracy, and it has embedded in children's minds the inspiring names and events of our history.

I have witnessed the growth of higher education until today our institutions of learning are turning out more instructed men and women each year than the rest of the world combined.

I have witnessed great discoveries from scientific research. With the advance of medical science, our youth are taller than their fathers, and the span of life has been greatly extended.

We can well respect the accomplishments of Russian technicians. But let us not forget that they obtained the telegraph, the telephone, the electric lamp, the speaking sound track, the radio broadcast tube, the airplane, atomic and nuclear power from us.

But with all these evidences of the future strength of America, I cannot say to you that we may be without fear. . . . . .

. . . . . In looking over the current scene in our national life, if we take a worm's-eye view of the crises and forces which surround us, we may worry that we are approaching the decline and fall of the greatest nation in history.

If we take a bird's-eye view, we see the fundamental strength of the American people.

And how can this strength be sustained and expanded?

It must come from growth of religious faith, from our devotion to freedom of men, and from a determined staunch stand against the evils which beset us. With these forces in motion, there can be no decline or fall in this nation.

But we have need to exert all the strengths which God has given our Nation.

CHAPLAIN'S CORNER

☆

by Rabbi Nathan Zelizer, 1958

Temple Tilfereth Israel, Columbus, Ohio
American Legion Post 430, Bexley, Ohio

☆

Almighty God, we thank Thee for life and its blessings. Inspire us so to live, think, and act as to preserve the good life, not only for ourselves but for future generations. Ever save us from conspiring to work evil. Save us from undue pride. Chase from our minds all impure thoughts. Stir within our souls compassion and love so that we may rejoicingly share life's blessings with the less fortunate. Keep us ever steadfast in the cause of the true and good life as taught by the sages and the prophets of the past, to the end that we may serve Thee without reproach and keep faith with all those who have made the supreme sacrifice for America where we have the freedom to live the good life. Amen.

WHAT IS AMERICA?

☆

by Sergeant Clement L. Lockwood

☆

It's the dream of billions of dreamers
Grown of seeds they have sown—
A symbol of hope for the future
Purchased in blood of their own.

It is more than a number of boundaries
And rivers so deep and so long;
It's a fortress blocking the pathway,
A barrier built against wrong.

It's more than its snow-capped mountains
And shores where the waves dash high;
It's a kerchief to dry up the tear drops,
A solace for those who cry.

It's more than its well-lighted cities
And its hustle and bustle by day;
It's the hope of the suffering masses
And the answer to those who pray.

It's more than a single great nation
With a Star Spangled Banner unfurled;
It's the rock that was planned at creation,
It's the hope of the whole wide world.

U. S. REAL PROMISED LAND TO OLD TIME IMMIGRANTS

☆

by *George E. Sokolsky*

1952

☆

My father was an immigrant from Bialystok, which was then in Russian Poland. I thought of that the other day when I received a pamphlet from our park department in New York with illustrations showing how they had beautified Battery Park. That was the first bit of America that my father saw when he landed on these shores from a steerage boat.

In his day, an old fortress there was called "Castle Garden," and the immigrants passed through it in hordes. That was when this country was in need of population and encouraged those who were hungry or frightened to come to America.

The most fantastic stories were told in Europe about the United States. To the immigrants, such as my father, it was a "goldene medina"—a "kingdom of gold." And literally, it was such, for while they lived in slums and worked unbelievably hard, their plight was better than anything they had known in the old country. And that is why they came here.

My father was a refugee from a pogrom. He ran away from social, economic, and spiritual deprivation. He wanted to worship God according to the traditions of his ancestors. He was a devotedly religious man, steeped in the lore of his faith, incapable of understanding life without it. Bread one could earn anywhere; liberty was hard to come by in his day.

Millions came, as he did, to build a new life in this country. I was brought up in this environment of hopeful people. They found life tough, particularly the adjustments of language and customs. And they suffered heartaches as their children moved away from them spiritually in the assimilative processes then catalyzing the sons and daughters of immigrants into Americans.

All of us were at least bi-lingual then. We spoke what was called the mother tongue, Yiddish, Russian, Polish, Italian, German, and whatnot. And we also spoke English, which our parents did not know, but which we got in the public schools and on the sidewalks. And there, too, we learned about the United States, its customs, its traditions, its institutions.

The children of those immigrants, first generation Americans, were jealous of their privileges. They were reared to regard the United States as a Promised Land. They were inspired in the schools to patriotic fervor. They were intolerant of anyone who even suggested that any other country could be equal to the United States. This was their country.

In later years, when times were better and young people went through school and college without hardship, when the third generation was living on the fat stored by their immigrant ancestors, they could not quite grasp the intensity of the emotions of the immigrants of the period be-

tween 1848 and 1890 for this country. The new generation were complainers; nothing was good enough for them.
But the old folks, they knew where they came from and
why and they were thankful.

My father never learned English. He lived in a ghetto
atmosphere by choice. He preferred to be among his own
kind and regarded it as a privilege to be able to do that
without fear. His greatest joy was the free practice of his
religion without danger or shame or humiliation. Yet, he
voted in every election and devoted himself to an understanding of the issues and the personalities about which he
read in the Yiddish newspapers which then flourished as
excellent journals. He was an independent in politics, as
were so many immigrants like himself. That was before the
politicians welded them into political blocs.

I am sure that no immigrant in those days ever thought
of himself as being part of a minority. They would not
have known what it meant. They were Americans. To have
called my father "a minority" would have been as insult-
ing as to call him a sheenie. He had run away from Europe
because there he was part of a minority; he came here because in America all people were Americans, all belonged
to the same Nation; all were equal in the eyes of the Government.

My father, the rabbi, and Father Louis, the priest, our
neighbor and friend, we were all the same kind of people
only we worshiped the same God differently. That he
could understand—but minority, pfui, that would have reminded him of the old country. That was no good.

"OLD GLORY"

☆

by C. S. Roberts, Jr.

☆

Anchored astern of us in Long Island Sound one summer evening was a luxurious yacht, while off to one side was an ancient, weather-beaten little craft with a ponderous man and a little boy—both in their undershirts—reposing in the cockpit.

At sundown, two uniformed sailors went to the stern of the yacht, fired a saluting cannon, and lowered the American flag. We had scarcely recovered from this display of grandeur when we heard another explosion off to port. Turning, we saw our friend in the undershirt holding a burst paper bag while the boy slowly lowered Old Glory.

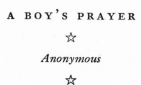

O God, on this day which is called the birthday of my country, I come to thee with joy and thankfulness in my heart. I thank thee for the courage and patience and faith which have been the possession of the real builders of my nation ever since the first explorers touched her shores. Help me to know that such qualities will always be greater than selfishness and greed and love of power.

I thank thee that I live in a land where knowledge is counted as a good thing and schools are free to all. May I be an intelligent citizen not only when I am grown to manhood but now as well.

O God, Creator of all beauty, thou hast made this country very beautiful! Far beyond imposing buildings and the ingenious inventions and conveniences which men have contrived do I prize steep mountains for my feet to climb, running streams to loiter beside, pine-carpeted forests in which dwell beasts and birds in their freedom. Help me to live near the things which thou hast made.

And because I am so proud of my country and her possibilities, because I am so thrilled to be a part of it all, may I realize that other boys in other countries have the same feelings. All the world is thine, O heavenly Father, and thou wouldst have us all be brothers. Let not pride of race or place of birth have room in my heart today, but let me in thought clasp hands with all boys the world around.

May I thus celebrate in truth my country's birthday. Amen.

☆

THE FLAG GOES BY

☆

by Henry Holcomb Bennett (1863-1924)

☆

Hats off!
Along the street there comes
A blare of bugles, a ruffle of drums,
A flash of color beneath the sky:
Hats off!
The flag is passing by!

Blue and crimson and white it shines,
Over the steel-tipped, ordered lines.
Hats off!
The colors before us fly;
But more than the flag is passing by.

Sea-fights and land-fights, grim and great,
Fought to make and to save the State:
Weary marches and sinking ships;
Cheers of victory on dying lips;

Days of plenty and years of peace;
March of a strong land's swift increase;
Equal justice, right and law,
Stately honor and reverend awe;

Sign of a nation, great and strong
To ward her people from foreign wrong:

Pride and glory and honor—all
Live in the colors to stand or fall.

Hats off!
Along the street there comes
A blare of bugles, a ruffle of drums;
And loyal hearts are beating high:
Hats off!
The flag is passing by!

THE BEST PATRIOTISM

☆

by Henry W. Grady

From "Against Centralization," speech to the Literary Societies
of the University of Virginia, June 25, 1889

☆

The germ of the best patriotism is in the love that a man
has for the home he inhabits, for the soil he tills, for the
trees that give him shade, and the hills that stand in his
pathway. I teach my son to love Georgia, to love the
soil that he stands on, the broad acres that hold her substance, the dimpling valleys in which her beauty rests, the
forests that sing her songs of lullaby and of praise, and the
brooks that run with her rippling laughter. The love of
home—deep-rooted and abiding—that blurs the eyes of the
dying soldier with the vision of an old homestead amid
green fields and clustering trees, that follows the busy man
through the clamoring world, persistent though put aside,
and at last draws his tired feet from the highway and leads
him through shady lanes and well-remembered paths until,
amid the scenes of his boyhood, he gathers up the broken
threads of his life and owns the soil his conqueror—this,
lodged in the heart of the citizen, is the saving principle
of our government.

We note the barracks of our standing army with its rolling drum and its fluttering flag as points of strength and
protection. But the citizen standing in the doorway of his
home, contented on his threshold, his family gathered about
his hearthstone while the evening of a well-spent day closes

in scenes and sounds that are dearest—he shall save the Republic when the drum tap is futile and the barracks are exhausted.

This love shall not be pent up or provincial. The home should be consecrated to humanity, and from its roof-tree should fly the flag of the Republic. Every simple fruit gathered there, every sacrifice endured, and every victory won should bring better joy and inspiration in the knowledge that it will deepen the glory of our Republic and widen the harvest of humanity!

Inherit without fear or shame the principle of local self-government by which your fathers stood! For that principle holds the imperishable truth that shall yet save this Republic. The integrity of the State, its rights and its powers—these, maintained with firmness, but in loyalty—these shall yet, by lodging the option of local affairs in each locality, meet the needs of this vast and complex government. The integrity of the States and the rights of the people! Stand there; there is safety; there is the broad and enduring brotherhood!

Exalt the citizen. As the State is the unit of government, he is the unit of the State. Teach him that his home is his castle, and his sovereignty rests beneath his hat. Make him self-respecting, self-reliant, and responsible. Let him lean on the State for nothing that his own arm can do, and on the government for nothing that his State can do. Let him cultivate independence to the point of sacrifice, and learn that humble things with unbartered liberty are better than splendors bought with its price. Let him neither surrender his individuality to government, nor merge it with the mob.

Let him stand upright and fearless—a freeman born of freemen, sturdy in his own strength, dowering his family in the sweat of his brow, loving to his State, loyal to his Republic, earnest in his allegiance wherever it rests, but building his altar in the midst of his household gods and shrining in his own heart the uttermost temple of its liberty.

Stand by these old-fashioned beliefs. Science hath revealed no better faith than that you learned at your mother's knee. Nor has knowledge made a wiser and a better book than the worn old Bible that, thumbed by hands long since still, and blurred with the tears of eyes long since closed, held the simple annals of your family and the heart and conscience of your homes.

Honor and emulate the virtues and the faith of your forefathers, who, learned, were never wise above a knowledge of God and His gospel; who, great, were never exalted above an humble trust in God and His mercy!

HOW IT BEGAN

☆

by Paul Harvey

From Remember These Things, *1952*

☆

When America's early pioneers first turned their eyes toward the West they did not demand that somebody take care of them if they got ill or got old. They did not demand maximum pay for minimum work, and even pay for no work at all. Come to think of it, they did not demand much of anything—except freedom.

They looked out at those rolling plains stretching away to the tall, green mountains, then lifted their eyes to the blue skies and said, "Thank you, God. I can take it from here."

☆

BOY HERO OF THE OREGON TRAIL

☆

by James H. Jauncey

1957

☆

Of all the heroic people who shared the danger of the Oregon trail one hundred years ago, the most courageous by far was a thirteen-year-old boy. Without the company of any grownups, he led his six brothers and sisters for five hundred miles through what is now Idaho and Oregon to the mouth of the Columbia River. At the time the forests were alive with Indians on the warpath, and all the way he had to carry in his arms an infant at the very point of death.

His name was John Sager. The family had come from the East with a wagon train heading for the wonderfully rich land to the west, known as the Oregon territory. As they approached Green River both parents became very ill and the wagon was forced to lag far behind the others.

When they reached the river, John had to take charge of everything. He took care of the tiny baby and fed the children. Then he built a great fire to keep them warm as he made preparations for the night. He was terribly worried about his mother and father who were now so sick that they could not move.

Suddenly there was a clattering of hoofs through the trees and a tall horseman in buckskin rode up.

"Put out that fire," ordered the stranger. "This is Sioux

country and they're out for paleface scalps. Where's your Pa and Ma?"

"They're sick," said John. "I'm in charge. What should I do?"

"Keep the children under cover and head in as fast as you can to join the others. I'll try and protect your rear. By the way, I'm Kit Carson."

John was thrilled when he heard that magic name. He had met the great Indian scout in person! Quickly he got the wagon rolling and hurried on. The oxen seemed to travel like snails. At every turn in the trail he expected Indians to appear. Every sound in the trees held a threat. The others were asleep and he was alone. He prayed to God for protection and pressed on.

By the time he caught up with the wagon train his parents were lying very still. The baby was sick for want of food. John was terribly alarmed. He handed the wagon over to his eleven-year-old brother, Francis, and ran ahead.

"I need a doctor," he yelled. "A doctor, my Pa and Ma are real bad."

"We don't have a doctor," said one man. "But I'm a vet. I'll see if I can help."

The veterinary climbed up into the Sager wagon while the people gathered around. In a moment he was out again and his face was grim.

"They're both dead," he said.

John felt a terrible cold feeling come all over him. "Oh, no!" he said. "They can't be! Not Pa and Ma, dead?"

He cried as if his heart would break. After a while he

dried his tears. There was work to do. He was the father now.

Kind women offered to take over the baby girl for him, but John refused. She was his little sister. They taught him to feed the weeks-old infant and the journey was resumed.

Now they kept with the rest of the wagon train and they reached Fort Hall, where they found a Hudson Bay Company trading station. Here they were warned of dangers ahead. A trader said that the mountains were impassable for wagons and advised the group to head south for California instead. After some consultation the leaders of the wagon train agreed to do as he suggested.

John was bitterly disappointed. His father had wanted the family to go to the Columbia River. John remembered how he had said that only a large number of American settlers could save the Oregon Territory for the United States, since the British also wanted it. He just couldn't go to California and let Dad down. He had to go on.

Without saying anything to his fellow travelers, John sold the wagon, keeping just the oxen to carry the pack and a cow for the baby's milk. Then he headed west with the family. Every night he prayed to God for help to bring them through.

Mile after mile they trudged, John ahead with the baby in his arms, the oxen and cow next, usually with children on their backs as well as packs. Finally, Francis brought up the rear. Most of the journey now was along the Snake River which they had to cross several times. This was terribly dangerous, but John always made sure the crossings were made at the safest places. Often they had to stop while they hunted for food. Sometimes days went by with hardly anything at all to eat.

Weeks went by. John was worried most about the baby. She was such a frail little thing. She did not cry like most babies, just lay in his arms very still.

At long last they came to Fort Boise. John hurried ahead with the baby and asked the trader for help. He was a great rough Scotchman, but with a kind heart. Tears came into his eyes when he saw the little ragamuffins. Their clothes were in shreds and their cheeks sunken with hunger.

He advised John to let an Indian woman nurse the baby. John refused, for he had heard that diseases could be caught that way. The trader warned him that it looked as if she might die. John then prayed,

"Please, God, don't let my little sister die."

The trader tried hard to persuade John not to cross over the treacherous Blue Mountains. But John wouldn't give in. When the friendly Scotchman saw that Sager was determined to go on, he gave him horses and hired two Indian guides to show them the way.

John was very grateful and with a lighter heart he continued his journey. But alas! One night the guides stole off in the darkness taking the horses with them. It was a bitter blow to the little family, but John would not turn back.

One day a terrible accident occurred. The eight-year-old girl slipped off the ox she was riding and broke her leg. All John could do was to pack it tight with snowballs and ask another sister to ride behind her.

The mountains were cold, and soon snow covered the

ground. Since the oxen and the cow were no longer able to get grass, John decided that he would have to abandon at least the oxen. He knew he must keep the cow for the baby's milk. With his bare hands he would dig away the snow so that the cow could graze on the grass underneath. The injured girl rode the cow.

For warmth, John wrapped the children in the tattered blankets that they still had and in the skins of the animals he was able to hunt and kill. The baby he kept rolled up in a wolf skin. At night he built huge fires so that they would not freeze to death while they slept.

On and on they trudged, their feet sore and bloody, their bodies cold and painful, their stomachs aching for food.

Now John had only one great goal and that was to reach the medical mission which he had been told was over the mountains. There the baby could get well and his sister's leg could be taken care of.

At last the highest ridge was climbed and they began the descent toward the valley of the Columbia River. When John first saw it, his heart filled with joy. He hadn't let Dad down. He had brought the family through.

Then one day he saw smoke curling up above the trees. They had reached the Mission Station. They all cried and hugged one another as they staggered into the compound.

The missionaries, Doctor and Mrs. Marcus Whitman, rushed to meet them. Mrs. Whitman took the baby and cried when she saw the tiny frail body so terribly ill. While the doctor set the broken leg and gave the others a hot bath, she tended the baby. John could not bear to leave the baby; his eyes were full of anxiety.

At last the baby gave a tiny little squeak, the first sound
he had heard from her in weeks. She was going to live!
John could not contain himself for joy. He danced and
laughed and cried all at once.

Only one thing bothered John that night as he lay on
his bed. Now they had arrived, what were they going to
do? It will be all right, he assured himself. The Heavenly Father who has taken care of us so far will not leave
us now.

He was right. The very next day the doctor told them
how their own baby girl had been drowned in the river
and they felt that God had sent the Sager children to take
her place. Yes! They would adopt all of them as their own
children.

John jerked his long red hair back out of his eyes and
grinned. "Thanks, Dr. Whitman," he said. "That's mighty
good of you. Thanks for Ma and Pa, too. They'd sure be
grateful to know the children would be taken care of."

THE COVERED WAGON

☆

by *Lena Whittaker Blakeney*

1929

☆

Through a mist of tears I watch the years
Of my youth go by again,
The golden years when the pioneers
First peopled an unknown plain.

By our campfire's gleam on a far-off stream,
Like a light in a drifting haze,
I journeyed back by the old dim track
That leads to the vanished days.

As the phantom trains of the wind-swept plains
In shadowy outlines pass,
The cottonwood trees stir with the breeze
That ripples the prairie grass.

The prairies swoon in the radiant noon,
And I catch the faint perfume
Of the cactus, blent with the faint sweet scent
Of the yucca's waxen bloom.

The cattle drink at the river's brink
At the close of the peaceful day;
They are dim-seen ghosts of the trampling hosts
That, far-flung, once held sway.

I hear the beat of a horse's feet,
And a note from a night-bird's throat,
The deadly purr of a rattler's whir,
And the bark of a lone coyote;

And the muffled thrum of the Indian drum
As it beats a weird tattoo
For the wild war dance—the old romance
Still stirs me through and through!

The trail grows dim . . . Ah, now the rim
Of the sunset sky bends low,
And the gray-green sedge at the prairie's edge
Is bathed in a blood-red glow!

The measured beat of my mustang's feet
Still lures me down the years,
And I want to ride back by the strong man's track
That I see tonight through tears.

THE NEW FRONTIER

☆

by John F. Kennedy

*From his acceptance of the Democratic nomination for President
at the National Convention in Los Angeles, July 15, 1960*

☆

I stand tonight facing west on what was once the last frontier. From the lands that stretch 3,000 miles behind me, the pioneers of old gave up their safety, their comfort, and sometimes their lives to build a new world here in the West.

. . . They were determined to make that new world strong and free, to overcome its hazards and its hardships, to conquer the enemies that threatened from without and within.

Today some would say that these struggles are all over —that all the horizons have been explored—that all the battles have been won—that there is no longer an American frontier.

But I trust that no one in this assemblage will agree with those sentiments. For the problems are not all solved and the battles are not all won—and we stand today on the edge of a new frontier—the frontier of the 1960's—a frontier of unknown opportunities and perils—a frontier of unfulfilled hopes and threats.

. . . The New Frontier of which I speak is not a set of promises—it is a set of challenges. It sums up not what I intend to offer the American people, but what I intend to ask of them. It appeals to their pride, not their pocketbook

—it holds out the promise of more sacrifice instead of more security.

But I tell you the New Frontier is here whether we seek it or not. Beyond that frontier are uncharted areas of science and space, unsolved problems of peace and war, unconquered pockets of ignorance and prejudice, unanswered questions of poverty and surplus.

. . . The times demand invention, innovation, imagination, decision. I am asking each of you to be new pioneers on that New Frontier. My call is to the young in heart regardless of age—to the stout in spirit, regardless of party—to all who respond to the scriptural call:

"Be strong and of good courage; be not afraid, neither be thou dismayed."

. . . We stand on this frontier at a turning-point in history. We must prove all over again whether this nation—or any nation so conceived—can long endure—whether our society—with its freedom of choice, its breadth of opportunity, its range of alternatives—can compete with the single-minded advance of the Communist system.

Can a nation organized and governed such as ours endure? That is the real question. Have we the nerve and the will? Can we carry through in an age where we will witness not only new breakthroughs in weapons of destruction—but also a race for mastery of the sky and the rain, the oceans and the tides, the far side of space and the inside of men's minds?

. . . All mankind waits upon our decision. A whole world looks to see what we will do. We cannot fail their trust; we cannot fail to try.

☆

MY CREED

☆

by Dean Alfange

Lawyer, *author of* The Supreme Court and the National Will

☆

I do not choose to be a common man. It is my right to be uncommon—if I can. I seek opportunity, not security. I do not wish to be a kept citizen, humbled and dulled by having the state look after me. I want to take the calculated risk, to dream and to build, to fail and to succeed. I refuse to barter incentive for a dole. I prefer the challenges of life to the guaranteed existence, the thrill of fulfillment to the stale calm of utopia.

I will not trade freedom for beneficence nor my dignity for a handout. I will never cower before any master nor bend to any threat. It is my heritage to stand erect, proud, and unafraid; to think and act for myself, enjoy the benefit of my creations, and to face the world boldly and say, this I have done.

All this is what it means to be an American.

☆

THE NIGHT IS NOT FOREVER

☆

A message of faith in the future from America's
Independent Electric Light and Power Companies, 1951

☆

In America, no night can last forever.

There is no darkness deep enough to hide for long the spirit of its people.

This is so because we have made it so.

Almost alone of all nations, we have held fast to our faith that every tomorrow holds the promise of a better life.

In America's long, hard march to greatness, its trials have brought it strength. From our wars we have won our freedoms. Panics have given way to serenity. Depressions have been followed by prosperity. From every night has come a dawn.

Now again the world is filled with fear and gloom. Once more, these are "times that try men's souls."

But let us not dread the dark. Let Americans keep alive their abiding faith in God, in our own tomorrow, and in ourselves.

That faith will be a tower of strength to the free world as it seeks to build a future.

☆

NOTHING TO FEAR

☆

by Franklin D. Roosevelt
From Inaugural Address, March 4, 1933

☆

. . . . . This great Nation will endure as it has endured.
. . . . . The only thing we have to fear is fear itself.
. . . . . We face the arduous duties that lie before us in
the warm courage of national unity; with the clear consciousness of seeking old and precious moral values; with
the clean satisfaction that comes from the stern perform-
ance of duty by old and young alike.

AMERICAN LITANY

☆

by Drew Brown
United States Coast Guard, World War II

☆

I hear America praying
A litany of people at war.
I hear America praying
From shore to distant shore.

The prayer of a brave, staunch People
With the faith of its Fathers strong.
I hear it loud and valiant,
It rings like a battle song.

Deep sprung from the heart of a nation
That sings as it faces the right
To rid the earth of the tyrant,
And prays to its God for the might

To stay the hand of the Vandal,
To bring peace on earth to all men.
Yes, this is the prayer of the People,
I hear it again and again.

I hear America praying
In a teeming tenement high.
A man . . . and his wife . . . and his child
Lift their voices and speak to the sky:

☆

"We thank thee, O God, for this great gift
Of a land where all men are one;
Please show us the way our hands may speed
Swift Victory early won."

I hear America praying—
A Negro . . . a hoe . . . and a field,
Soil on his hands and sweat on his brow,
A smile his inviolate shield:

"This task, O Lord, is my job, too;
And staked out well is my share
To draw from the flowing breast of the earth,
Strength for the men out there."

I hear America praying
In a fox-hole pounded with rain,
The smoke of war in his nostrils,
His eye on a hovering plane:

"I don't ask much for me, O Lord,
I'll come through this all somehow,
But the ones at home . . . Watch over them!
Dear Lord, they're Your job now."

I hear America praying—
A mother writing at night
Heart'ning word to a son on a nameless sea
With fear in her heart locked tight:

"Please help him be brave, dear God,
And in faith treat fear with disdain;
And, if it be Thy will, he returns not to me,
Let his offering have been not in vain."

I hear America praying—
The rhythm of rivets its score—
The prayer of a man in his shirt sleeves,
Never raising his eyes from his chore:

"O Banish all quarrel and selfish harangue,
Today has no leisure. Time runs.
God grant us one aim and one holy creed:
More ships, more planes, and more guns."

This, then, O God, is the prayer I hear
Surging on to a great Amen.
This is the prayer America prays,
I hear it again and again.

☆

CONVERSATION BETWEEN INTIMATES

☆

by B. Y. Williams

1943

☆

"These are dark days,"
Said the body,
"The life that we loved has gone;
America's dream is shattered
And joy is done."

"These are bright days,"
Said the spirit,
"Now heroes inhabit the earth;
America's soul is tested
And proves its worth."

CHRISTMAS, 1942

☆

by Emmet Fox

from Make Your Life Worthwhile

☆

Christmas has come around once more, and we find the nation passing through a time of great testing. Today the American people are called upon to prove their faith in God, and in those American principles which are written in our Constitution.

The response has been magnificent. Every section of the community has demonstrated its unshakable resolve to make every effort toward the great Victory that we know will be ours.

People do not speak of making "sacrifices" today, for we feel that to forego, temporarily, some of our liberties and some of our comforts, is a privilege and a high honor.

Above all, we who have the Jesus Christ teaching rejoice in the knowledge that we can help those we love with our prayers, realizing that they who dwell in the secret place abide in the shadow of the Almighty and that they can throw the protection of their prayers around their loved ones.

Let us in the coming year keep the Ninety-first Psalm very close to our hearts.

PSALM 91

He that dwelleth in the secret place of the most High shall abide under the shadow of the Almighty.

I will say of the Lord, *He is* my refuge and my fortress: my God; in him will I trust.

Surely he shall deliver thee from the snare of the fowler, *and* from the noisome pestilence.

He shall cover thee with his feathers, and under his wings shalt thou trust: his truth *shall be thy* shield and buckler.

Thou shalt not be afraid for the terror by night; *nor* for the arrow *that* flieth by day;

Nor for the pestilence *that* walketh in darkness; *nor* for the destruction *that* wasteth at noonday.

A thousand shall fall at thy side, and ten thousand at thy right hand; *but* it shall not come nigh thee.

Only with thine eyes shalt thou behold and see the reward of the wicked.

Because thou hast made the Lord, *which is* my refuge, *even* the most High, thy habitation;

There shall no evil befall thee, neither shall any plague come nigh thy dwelling.

For he shall give his angels charge over thee, to keep thee in all thy ways.

They shall bear thee up in *their* hands, lest thou dash thy foot against a stone.

Thou shalt tread upon the lion and adder: the young lion and the dragon shalt thou trample under feet.

Because he hath set his love upon me, therefore will I deliver him: I will set him on high, because he hath known my name.

He shall call upon me, and I will answer him: I *will be* with him in trouble; I will deliver him, and honour him.

With long life will I satisfy him, and shew him my salvation.

AMERICAN HERO NUMBER ONE

☆

Robert Gordon Smith
World War II

☆

My choice for American Hero Number One is the average American man or woman whose ancestry may date from the *Mayflower* or a naturalization ceremony. He may be from any nation on earth including those we fight, of any race or creed, but he is an American if America is where he wants to live and if he is willing to die for the preservation of its institutions.

There is more to heroism than a sudden glorious exploit. He is of the stuff of which heroes are made who does his daily job, whatever it is, because that is his job; who provides for his own and has something to spare for others; who tries to be decent, to get along with people, and to meet life's challenges; who, in time of war, is willing to serve where he may serve best, in uniform or old clothes, shedding his blood or sharing it with others; and who, without saying much about it, trusts in God.

Such a man is my choice because without millions like him there would be no America and no flashing stars to add new luster to the cause of Freedom and Justice for All.

REFLECTION OF A RED CROSS
BLOOD DONOR

☆

by *Gertrude Curtis Ryan*

☆

Strange that this blood which flows so easily
Out of my unprotesting, drug-soothed vein
Into its sterile flask, the while I chat
Of this and that, remote from strife or pain,
May, when the need in some far battle zone
Rises, to wrest from death some lithe-limbed boy,
Flow back with all its life-strong properties
And give him back to living and to joy.

Strange that my blood in quiet middle age,
Where long had cooled the singing, searching flame,
May, roused once again, to answer spring
In some new youth who will not know my name.
Some youth, now proud in battle uniform,
Fighting among the clouds, on land or sea,
For that old dream we dreamed at Valley Forge,
That all men might walk tall and straight and free.

A DUTY TO MANKIND

☆

by Theodore Roosevelt

From a Speech at Osawatomie, Kansas, August 31, 1910

☆

The history of America is now the central feature of the history of the world, for the world has set its face hopefully toward our democracy; and, O my fellow citizens, each one of you carries on your shoulders not only the burden of doing well for the sake of your own country, but the burden of doing well and of seeing that this nation does well for the sake of mankind.

LINES TO THE WOMEN OF AMERICA

☆

by *A. B. Purdie*
Chaplain, R.A.F., 1944

☆

Here in this precious isle,
Scarred bastion of a challenged world,
Or lapped in mist,
Or kissed
By fitful suns of the fast-falling year,
Your boys,
Great-hearted, generous, and true,
Are gathered to our hearts awhile,
And held
In trust for you.

Held for a little while:
We know we cannot keep
Their inmost hearts,
Hearts that are yours inseparably.
Could your fond eyes
Cheat distances and overleap
The barrier of the estranging deep,
You'd see
Beyond their play
Of laughter and gay gallantry,
Their souls adream
In wistful longing for the ones they love,
So far, so far away!

Not long
Their sojourn on these distant fields,
On murmurous shores, where sea gulls call,
In rosy hamlets, or by copse and stream,
Or where the golden orchards gleam
By humble cot and stately hall . . .
Not long:
For soon the tide of victory shall flow,
And healing waters surging in
Shall every tortured acre fill
And cleanse a festering world of ill:
And flood
And overwhelm
The murky fastnesses of sin!

☆

by Robert Montgomery

*Address to the fifty-sixth annual Congress of American Industry,
sponsored by the National Association of Manufacturers
December, 1951*

☆

When in the course of human events, inhuman forces arise to threaten freedom, we who still are free arise to defend it.

We have met the challenge before and beaten it down. We have learned the need for unending vigilance. We are vigilant now. We are united, determined, and strong.

This is not alone because of our material strength: our real power flows from our moral and spiritual resources. We are strong because we are free, and we have been bred to value freedom far above our lives. We pride ourselves on certain traditions, certain values.

As free men we believe in the tradition of individualism —in the integrity of the individual, his personal worth, his independence, his dignity. We believe in the widest personal opportunity, narrowed down as little as possible by public interference. We believe in the competitive spirit— in competition among ourselves, but not between the governed and those who govern. We believe in free private enterprise—in what a man can achieve by his own hands and brain, by his energy, industry, and inspiration, by his determination and self-reliance.

As free men we believe in the other fellow's freedom—

in his merit, his integrity and his independence. We believe in the tradition of mutual self-help. And we endorse the practice, as well as the theory, of the Golden Rule. We believe in the tradition of decentralized power, politically and economically.

As free men we believe in a rule of law and in a government of laws rather than of men. That is because where laws rule, impartial justice is probable; where men rule, partial justice is possible.

As free men we believe in the right of democratic criticism of authority; we reject thought control as well as speech control. We seek the truth but reserve the right to be honestly mistaken.

These traditions, these values, these freedoms form the great and unshakable foundation of our system.

We have learned to recognize the enemy within or without. We can peer through his smokescreen; we know all his tricks of camouflage.

He may appear in a different uniform. He may run up different colors. He may sound a new battle cry of hate. But he can never change his true identity. This enemy is always tyranny—whether imperialism in 1914, Naziism in 1941, or Communism today.

In earlier trials the cause of freedom emerged triumphant over the soul-destroying forces that blocked the human path. We who were rescued from tyranny then do not forget the rescuers who fought and the rescuers who died. We who still are free will conquer again—in their name, and in the name of freedom.

TO BRING THEM PEACE

*A Message from Our Soldiers in Korea to the Folks
Back Home*

☆

by Francis Cardinal Spellman, 1953

☆

Soldiers in Korea,
What shall you say to us who live in peace,
While you by war's uncertain fate are bound?

I read an answer in each upturned face
Or lowered head while I, in sacrifice
And prayer, with you beg God to bring men peace—
An answer, varied as the instruments
That make an orchestra, each vibrant with
Its own true note, yet weaving into one
Great harmony that swells and cresting, breaks
Upon the harkening ear, or as great waves
That rhythmic beat, drum-like, upon a shore
Beneath the baton of a hurricane.

And here within mine anguished soul I catch
This answer, which your many-throated voice
Cries out to me. Just as our dead cry out
From muted lips, with eloquence you cry:
"We did not wish to fight, yet fight we did!
Reluctantly we left our native shores,
By duty called to serve our country's cause

☆

And take up battle in these somber hills;
But it is now our firm, unwavering will
To carry on, determined to keep faith
With them who sacrificed themselves for us.
The blood and price they gave was limitless,
Who gave their all. Never will we betray
That trust! Our dead shall never taunt the living
Because what they had saved for us was lost.

We are not happy in this bloody strife,
We long to share the luxury of peace,
The blessed bounties Peace holds in her lap.
It is for our own children that we fight,
For wives, parents, and friends, for all that binds
The soul of man to man and man to God.
To guard these sacred gifts, bestowed on us
By Him we call 'Our Father,' we now bend
To this dread task, with hope and fervent prayer
That we may live to see our homes again
And feel beneath our feet our native earth.

Please tell the folks back home we struggle on
With courage born of hope for better days
And better ways of life than now we know;
With faith, that deep beneath the mirth and play
The airways bring us from the far-off States,
There stirs a mighty nation's gratitude.
We shall not fail *our* sacred trust—*and yours*—
Nor leave 'democracy' a graven word
Upon a tombstone, in a prison world."

Soldiers in Korea,
How shall I answer you, whose eyes search mine?
With the strict truth—and pray you understand:
The folks back home are wakened to your need.
Since you are blood of ours, you know full well
How slowly men of peace prepare for war:
Repeated blows must forge the shining blade,
A maze of plots quicken our laggard wills;
The studied insults of a well-armed foe
But tardily have 'roused our nation's soul,
And loosed us from our dreams of hard-earned peace;
A people whose strong heart abhorreth war
Now humbly girds itself in just defense,
Geared to do battle for those precious gifts
Whose sum is liberty. Despite delays,
Pray count the folks back home as one with you,
Solicitous to succor all your needs.
Admiring you, we offer deepest thanks;
Revering you, we offer our hearts' love,
Defenders, saviours of our country's life!

☆

Human Nature, Preferred

☆

New York World-Telegram, 1945

☆

A few months after William Hallicy, New Jersey nursery-man, joined the Seabees in February, 1942, a brush fire swept his four-acre plot. When he went home the other day after being discharged, he found his nursery was nothing but weeds and charred trees. Nurseryman Hallicy figured it would take him eight years to grow salable stock from seedlings. He was planning to raise chickens and turkeys until his nursery could produce again.

But nurseryman Hallicy had not figured on his neighborhood competitors. Members of the North Jersey Nurserymen's Association got together and agreed that "a man who was good enough to sacrifice his business to fight for his country deserved a new start."

Unannounced, they appeared at the Hallicy home with $2,500 worth of small trees in fifteen trucks. With tractor, plow, and spades they cleared the plot and set out the trees. In a few hours the Hallicy nursery was right smack back in business. Neighbor Hallicy stared and gulped. He finally managed to pull himself together and serve beer. But nothing could wash down the lump in his throat.

We understand the lump in the Hallicy throat. We're getting one of our own, just thinking about his neighbors. Makes us want to go right out and buy a big flock of stock in human nature, common and preferred.

Our Friendly Guardians

☆

H. F. W. in the Christian Science Monitor

☆

Motorists driving along a certain busy highway one day fretted impatiently when the traffic policeman halted the heavy traffic. There seemed no reason for the delay, as far as they could see.

Then they heard the policeman call out, "Hurry up, Jackie. Come on now." And at that moment a small squirrel scampered out from beneath a clump of bushes with a nut in his mouth. As the little animal paused at the edge of the sidewalk, the officer coaxed, "Now, hurry up, Jackie." Obediently the squirrel dashed across the street with a flourish of his tail which seemed to convey a "thank you" for the officer's protection.

The scene lasted only a moment. But it was long enough for impatient frowns to change to friendly grins of appreciation as the motorists set out once more with a new feeling of interest in that particular guardian of traffic.

Americans Never Stop Giving

☆

Associated Press

☆

An Atlanta woman, riding home on a bus, suddenly realized she had left a "piggy bank" at the post office while mailing letters. She hurried back and found the bank on the counter, but noticed it had become heavier.

Generous Atlantans, thinking it was there for aiding some worthy cause, had put many coins in it.

Never A Hug So Tight

☆

American Airlines

1952

☆

She was only ten years old, but feeling mighty grown up about crossing the country on an airplane all by herself. Then, just before she arrived in New York, she suddenly became a scared little girl. For they were gone! She'd lost them! Lost the three dollars that were her entire capital. Lost the precious ticket that would take her on to Boston —and home.

That is why our chief agent, Joe Croasdale, who met the plane that day found one small passenger leaving the

Flagship with tears streaming down her cheeks. But as soon as she explained her troubles, the tears gave way to smiles.

For the chief agent was a father himself. He bought another ticket immediately, then dug down into his own pocket for three dollars and gravely replenished the small traveler's capital. Never was a kiss so grateful! Never was a hug so tight!

☆

OUR WAY OF LIFE

☆

by *Wendell L. Willkie* (*1892-1944*)

From One World, *1943*

☆

Our way of living together in America is a strong but delicate fabric. It is made up of many threads. It has been woven over many centuries by the patience and sacrifice of countless liberty-loving men and women. It serves as a cloak for the protection of poor and rich, of black and white, of Jew and Gentile, of foreign- and native-born.

Let us not tear it asunder. For no man knows, once it is destroyed, where or when man will find its protective warmth again.

I SPOKE UP AT TOWN MEETING

☆

Republic Steel Corporation, 1951

☆

". . . . . something I didn't like about the way town funds were being spent. I'm not much of a guy for making speeches, understand . . . I just work in a steel mill. . . . . .

"But nobody beat me up! Now, you might say, what's so unusual about me not getting beat up for speaking out against the local government?

"That's just my point . . . it isn't unusual! Not in this country. Here we all have free speech. It's part of our Constitution, even if we hardly ever think about it twice. But just think of the folks in other countries . . . billions of 'em, maybe . . . who'd give their right eye to be American citizens and talk out at town meetings. Or, if they want, from a soapbox. And *not* get slugged.

"Ever stop to think that while all these people are trying to get *into* America, nobody here is trying to get *out?* That's because we like it here. No, not just because we've got autos and phones and bathtubs and all that. The real reason is . . . we've got Freedom! Seven days a week! We're free to follow our own religions . . . free to choose our own jobs in any industry we like . . . or go into business for ourselves, if we prefer. We can vote as we please . . . or not vote, if we want. Though I personally think anyone who doesn't is a fourteen-carat dope.

"And here, like I said, you can talk up at Town Meeting.

No black eye. No bloody nose. Though, if you don't know what you're talking about, you'll be in for a lot of kidding later.

"Now this is no Town Meeting, of course . . . it's an ad. But, in this ad, I am speaking up . . . for Freedom. Corny? Maybe . . . but I happen to believe in it. And ten to one you do, too!"

Republic became strong in a strong and free America. Republic can remain strong only in an America that remains strong and free . . . an America whose many mighty industries have set history's highest standard of living for her people.

Some people think that America is all skyscrapers and chromium fittings and elegant plumbing; some people think it's all bankers and brokers and Big Business; some people think it's all sharecroppers and Oakies and erosion. And some people think it's all cowboys and Indians; some people think it's all gangsters; some people think it's all movie stars; some people think America is Fifth Avenue and some people think it's Main Street and some people think it's Catfish Row.

Some people think it's the Little Red Schoolhouse and the Old Swimming Hole and the frame house and the back porch and the cluster of little gray mailboxes leaning toward each other on crooked posts by the side of long, straight roads—and these people perhaps come nearer to the truth than most.

But even those haven't got at the whole truth. They are all wrong, and yet they are all right. The truth is that America is the Constitution, and the Constitution is America. The Constitution is at once the source and the distillation of this country. It is what makes all these varied Americas possible. Some of them are good and some of them are bad, but the great point is that because of the Constitution, the bad ones are capable of being made good, and the good ones are capable of being made perfect.

☆

The Constitution is what gives freedom and flexibility to the whole vast setup; the Constitution is what gives the country unity without uniformity, and that is the most priceless gift that any country can have.

CHARTER OF FREEDOM

☆

Robert Gordon Smith

☆

Thank God for the noble men who through a long, trying summer wrote that magnificent document of human dignity and freedom—the Constitution of the United States of America. And thank God, too, for those wonderful women whose gracious hospitality on many a hot summer evening did so much to soothe ruffled tempers and bring disputing delegates together, paving the way for better understanding and mutual appreciation of differing viewpoints. Thus the ladies of Philadelphia served along with the delegates in bulding a worthy charter of freedom for the new nation brought forth in that same Independence Hall just eleven years before.

September 17, 1962, marks the 175th anniversary of that memorable occasion for all mankind when George Washington, President of the Constitutional Convention, signed his name to the final draft, followed by the delegates from twelve of the original thirteen states. Benjamin Franklin, Alexander Hamilton, and James Madison are, perhaps, the best known today of the other thirty-eight signers, but all richly deserve our gratitude and praise for a monumental task.

The excerpts from the Constitution that follow define the principal functions of the government's executive, legislative, and judicial branches, and indicate the rights and powers guaranteed to individual citizens and the states respectively. God grant that each true American—young or old, rich or poor, of every trade, profession, race, creed, and station in life—re-dedicate himself to a better knowledge of, appreciation for, and devotion to our American Constitution in preference to all other political documents. The Constitution, with its first ten amendments—our Bill of Rights—is far more advanced than the political ideas and social theories, so alien to the American way of life, that some would foolishly foist upon us.

Let us consecrate our best efforts during the twenty-five years from 1962 to 1987 to a revitalization of that charter of freedom our forefathers so laboriously, farsightedly and courageously brought forth. Then we will be able to fittingly celebrate the two hundredth anniversary of the Constitution in joyous but solemn awareness that we have kept the faith for which our fathers lived and died.

We can, indeed, go forward gloriously by taking "Back to the Constitution" as our battle cry. And with us will go the hopes of all the world for a brighter day of human dignity, freedom, and brotherhood under God, the eternal Creator of all.

THE CONSTITUTION OF THE UNITED STATES

☆

WE THE PEOPLE of the United States, in order to form a more perfect union, establish justice, insure domestic tranquillity, provide for the common defense, promote the general welfare, and secure the blessings of liberty to ourselves and our posterity, do ordain and establish this Constitution for the United States of America.

ARTICLE I

Section 1. All legislative Powers herein granted shall be vested in a Congress of the United States, which shall consist of a Senate and a House of Representatives.

Section 7. All Bills for raising Revenue shall originate in the House of Representatives; but the Senate may propose or concur with Amendments as on other Bills.

Every Bill which shall have passed the House of Representatives and the Senate, shall, before it become a Law, be presented to the President of the United States; If he approve he shall sign it, but if not he shall return it, with his Objections to that House in which it shall have originated, who shall enter the Objections at large on their journal and proceed to reconsider it. If after such Reconsideration two thirds of that House shall agree to pass the Bill, it shall be sent, together with the Objections, to the other House, by which it shall likewise be reconsidered, and if approved by two thirds of that House, it shall become a Law. . . . . . If any Bill shall not be returned by the President within ten Days (Sundays excepted) after it shall have been presented to him, the Same shall be a Law, in like Manner as if he had signed it, unless the Congress by their Adjournment prevent its Return, in which Case it shall not be a Law.

Every Order, Resolution, or Vote to which the Concurrence of the Senate and the House of Representatives may be necessary (except on a question of Adjournment) shall be presented to the President of the United States; and before the Same shall take Effect, shall be approved by him, or being disapproved by him, shall be repassed by two thirds of the Senate and the House of Representatives, according to the Rules and Limitations prescribed in the Case of a Bill.

Section 8. The Congress shall have Power to lay and collect Taxes, Duties, Imposts and Excises, to pay the Debts and provide for the common Defense and general Welfare of the United States; but all Duties, Imposts and Excises shall be uniform throughout the United States;

To borrow Money on the credit of the United States;

To regulate Commerce with foreign Nations, and among the several States and with the Indian Tribes;

To establish an uniform Rule of Naturalization and uniform Laws on the subject of Bankruptcies throughout the United States;

To coin Money, regulate the Value thereof, and of foreign Coin, and fix the Standard of Weights and Measures;

To provide for the Punishment of counterfeiting the Securities and current coin of the United States;

To establish Post Offices and Post Roads;

To promote the Progress of Science and useful Arts, by securing for limited times to Authors and Inventors the exclusive Right to their respective Writings and Discoveries;

To constitute Tribunals inferior to the supreme Court;

To define and punish Piracies and Felonies committed on the high Seas and Offenses against the Law of Nations;

To declare War, grant Letters of Marque and Reprisal, and make Rules concerning Captures on Land and Water;

To raise and support Armies, but no appropriation of Money to that Use shall be for a longer Term than two years;

To provide and maintain a Navy;

To make rules for the Government and Regulation of the land and naval forces;

To provide for calling forth the Militia to execute the Laws of the Union, suppress Insurrections and repel Invasions;

To provide for organizing, arming, and disciplining the militia, ...

To exercise exclusive Legislation in all Cases whatsoever, over such District (not exceeding ten Miles square) as may, by Cession of particular States, and the Acceptance of Congress, become the seat of the Government of the United States, and to exercise like Authority over all Places purchased by the Consent of the Legislature of the State in which the Same shall be, for the Erection of Forts, Magazines, Arsenals, dock-Yards, and other needful Buildings;— And

To make all Laws which shall be necessary and proper for carrying into execution the foregoing powers, and all other Powers vested by this Constitution in the Government of the United States, or in any Department or Officer thereof.

Section 10. No state shall enter into any Treaty, Alliance, or Confederation; grant Letters of Marque and Reprisal; coin Money; emit Bills of Credit; make any Thing but gold and silver Coin a Tender in Payment of Debts; pass any Bill of Attainder, ex post facto Law, or Law impairing the Obligation of Contracts, or grant any Title of Nobility.

No State shall, without the Consent of the Congress, lay any Imposts or Duties on Imports or Exports, except what may be absolutely necessary for executing its inspection Laws; and the net Produce of all Duties and Imposts laid by any State on Imports or Exports, shall be for the Use of the Treasury of the United States; and all such Laws shall be subject to the Revision and Control of the Congress.

No State shall, without the Consent of Congress, lay any Duty of Tonnage, keep Troops, or Ships of War in time of Peace, enter into any Agreement or Compact with another State, or with a foreign Power, or engage in War, unless actually invaded, or in such imminent Danger as will not admit of delay.

Section 1. The executive Power shall be vested in a President of the United States of America. . . . . .

Section 2. The President shall be Commander in Chief of the Army and Navy of the United States, and of the Militia of the several States, when called into the actual Service of the United States; he may require the Opinion, in writing, of the principal Officer in each of the executive Departments, upon any Subject relating to the Duties of their respective Offices, and he shall have Power to grant Reprieves and Pardons for Offenses against the United States, except in Cases of Impeachment.

He shall have Power, by and with the Advice and Consent of the Senate to make Treaties, provided two thirds of the Senators present concur; and he shall nominate, and by and with the Advice and Consent of the Senate, shall appoint Ambassadors, other public Ministers and Consuls, Judges of the supreme Court, and all other Officers of the United States, whose Appointments are not herein otherwise provided for, and which shall be established by Law: but the Congress may by Law vest the Appointment of such inferior Officers as they think proper, in the President alone, in the courts of Law, or in the Heads of Departments.

The President shall have Power to fill up all Vacancies that may happen during the Recess of the Senate, by granting Commissions which shall expire at the End of their next Session.

Section 3. He shall from time to time give to the Congress Information of the State of the Union, and recommend to their Consideration such Measures as he shall judge necessary and expedient; he may, on extraordinary Occasions, convene both Houses, or either of them . . . . . he shall take Care that the Laws be faithfully executed. . . . . .

Section 4. The President, Vice President, and all civil Officers of the United States, shall be removed from Office on Impeachment for, and Conviction of, Treason, Bribery, or other high Crimes and Misdemeanors.

ARTICLE III

Section 1. The judicial Power of the United States shall be vested in one supreme Court, and in such inferior Courts as the Congress may from time to time ordain and establish. . . . . .

Section 2. The judicial Power shall extend to all Cases, in Law and Equity, arising under this Constitution, the Laws of the United States, and Treaties made, or which shall be made, under their Authority;—to all Cases affect-

ing Ambassadors, other public Ministers and Consuls;—
to all Cases of admiralty and maritime Jurisdiction;—to
Controversies to which the United States shall be a Party;
—to Controversies between two or more States;—between
a State and Citizens of another State;—between Citizens of
different States;—between Citizens of the same State claim-
ing Lands under Grants of different States, and between a
State, or the Citizens thereof, and foreign States, Citizens
or Subjects.

In all cases affecting Ambassadors, other public Ministers
and Consuls, and those in which a State shall be Party, the
supreme Court shall have original Jurisdiction. In all the
other Cases before mentioned, the supreme Court shall
have appellate Jurisdiction, both as to Law and Fact, with
such Exceptions, and under such Regulations as the Congress shall make.

The Trial of all Crimes, except in Cases of Impeachment, shall be by Jury;. . . . . .

ARTICLE IV

Section 1. Full Faith and Credit shall be given in each
State to the public Acts, Records, and judicial Proceedings
of every other State. . . . . .

Section 2. The Citizens of each State shall be entitled to
all Privileges and Immunities of Citizens in the several
States. . . . . .

Section 3. New States may be admitted by the Congress into this Union; . . . . .

Section 4. The United States shall guarantee to every State in this Union a Republican Form of Government, and shall protect each of them against Invasion; and on Application of the Legislature, or of the Executive (when the Legislature cannot be convened) against domestic Violence.

ARTICLE VI

All Debts contracted and Engagements entered into, before the Adoption of this Constitution, shall be as valid against the United States under this Constitution, as under the Confederation.

This Constitution, and the Laws of the United States which shall be made in Pursuance thereof; and all Treaties made, or which shall be made, under the authority of the United States, shall be the supreme Law of the land; and the judges in every State shall be bound thereby, any Thing in the Constitution or Laws of any State to the contrary notwithstanding.

The Senators and Representatives before mentioned, and the Members of the several State Legislatures, and all executive and judicial Officers, both of the United States and of the several States, shall be bound by Oath or Affirmation, to support this Constitution; but no religious Test shall ever be required as a qualification to any Office or public Trust under the United States.

ARTICLE VII

The Ratification of the Conventions of nine States, shall be sufficient for the Establishment of this Constitution between the States so ratifying the same.

Done in Convention by the Unanimous Consent of the States present, the Seventeenth Day of September in the Year of our Lord one thousand seven hundred and Eighty-seven and of the Independence of the United States of America the Twelfth. In witness whereof, We have hereunto subscribed our Names.

AMENDMENTS

Article I. Congress shall make no law respecting an establishment of religion, or prohibiting the free exercise thereof; or abridging the freedom of speech, or of the press; or the right of the people peaceably to assemble, and to petition the Government for a redress of grievances.

Article II. A well regulated Militia, being necessary to the security of a free State, the right of the people to keep and bear Arms, shall not be infringed.

Article III. No Soldier shall, in time of peace be quartered in any house, without the consent of the Owner, nor in time of war, but in a manner to be prescribed by law.

Article IV. The right of the people to be secure in their persons, houses, papers, and effects, against unreasonable searches and seizures, shall not be violated, and no Warrants shall issue, but upon probable cause, supported by Oath or affirmation, and particularly describing the place to be searched, and the persons or things to be seized.

Article V. No person shall be held to answer for a capital, or otherwise infamous crime, unless on a presentment or indictment of a Grand Jury, except in cases arising in the land or naval forces, or in the Militia, when in actual service in time of war or public danger; nor shall any person be subject for the same offense to be twice put in jeopardy of life or limb; nor shall be compelled in any Criminal Case to be a witness against himself, nor be deprived of life, liberty or property, without due process of law; nor shall private property be taken for public use, without just compensation.

Article VI. In all criminal prosecutions, the accused shall enjoy the right to a speedy and public trial, by an impartial jury of the State and district wherein the crime shall have been committed, which district shall have been previously ascertained by law, and to be informed of the nature and cause of the accusation; to be confronted with the witnesses against him; to have compulsory process for obtaining witnesses in his favor, and to have the assistance of counsel for his defense.

Article VII. In suits at common law, where the value in controversy shall exceed twenty dollars, the right of trial by jury shall be preserved, and no fact tried by a jury shall be otherwise re-examined in any Court of the United States than according to the rules of the common law.

Article VIII. Excessive bail shall not be required, nor excessive fines imposed, nor cruel and unusual punishments inflicted.

Article IX. The enumeration in the Constitution of certain rights shall not be construed to deny or disparage others retained by the people.

Artcile X. The powers not delegated to the United States by the Constitution, nor prohibited by it to the States, are reserved to the States respectively, or to the people.

The above ten amendments, known as the Bill of Rights, took effect in December, 1791. Additional amendments have been added through the years, as follows:

Eleven: The Judicial power of the United States shall not be construed to extend to any suit in law or equity, commenced or prosecuted against one of the United States by Citizens of another State, or by Citizens or Subjects of any Foreign State.

Twelve clarifies the procedure for electing the President and Vice President.

Thirteen abolished slavery.

Fourteen assures American citizenship to all persons born or naturalized in the United States, and subject to its jurisdiction. "No state shall make or enforce any law which shall abridge the privileges or immunities of citizens of the United States; nor shall any State deprive any person of life, liberty, or property without due process of law; nor deny to any person within its jurisdiction the equal protection of its laws."

Fifteen assures the right to vote to all citizens, regardless of race or color.

Sixteen legalizes a federal tax on income.

Seventeen provides for election of Senators by direct vote of the people. (Until 1913 Senators were chosen by state legislatures.)

Eighteen established Prohibition.

Nineteen in effect gives women the right to vote.

Twenty changes the dates for the inauguration of the President and Vice President to January 20 and specifies that Congress shall assemble at least once a year.

Twenty-one repealed Prohibition.

Twenty-two forbids the election of any person as President more than twice.

A GOVERNMENT OF THE PEOPLE

☆

by John Marshall

Chief Justice of the United States Supreme Court, 1801-1835

☆

The government of the Union, then, is emphatically and truly a government of the people. In form and in substance it emanates from them. Its powers are granted by them, and are to be exercised directly on them and for their benefit.

From McCulloch vs. Maryland, *1819*

☆

GUARD THE CONSTITUTION

☆

by William LaVarre

1951

☆

Americans are plagued today by various political groups that want to change the Constitution of the United States. The Constitution, these groups insist, is "outmoded" and must be amended before we can go forward into a Bigger and Better Life. With persuasive arguments they seek to convince us that a little change here and there would improve and "streamline" the Constitution.

But what is the truth? The truth is that the Constitution of the United States is a great Gibraltar of human integrity, peace, and freedom, effectively blocking those who would enslave us from achieving their ultimate goals.

As we travel the world, we see constant proof that nowhere else in today's civilization does there exist a nation as great and powerful as the United States. No other country enjoys our luxuries of strength, wealth, freedom, prosperity, and security. Across the seas other powers have suffered political and economic defeat; many have become captive nations. How did it happen that the United States, beginning in a primitive wilderness, grew so strong, wealthy, and secure, while so many other nations began to wither and die? Was it just good luck?

The Chinese have an old proverb which says that the success of the longest journey begins with the first step. Our long journey as a nation began with a first step that

was both slow and laborious—the creation of a constitutional government for welding thriteen individualistic
states into a strong humanitarian union. Our first step was
taken by the American patriots who wrote out and pledged
allegiance to an agreed-upon document that history has
proven to be a colossal monument to human wisdom.

The secret of America's strength today lies in the miracle
that began one hundred sixty-three years ago, when on
September 17, 1787, delegates to the Constitutional Convention in Philadelphia signed the first step in our national
journey—the Constitution.

"We, the People . . . . ."

We, the People of the United States—for a century and
a half and in a world of constant antagonism—have grown
into more perfect union, established justice, insured domestic tranquillity, provided for the common defense, promoted the general welfare, and secured the blessings of
liberty to ourselves and our posterity. Strength came to us
from a strong Constitution, which, like a block of hardest
stone, adamantly refused to permit itself to be chipped to
pieces, generation after generation.

Had the people of the United States been easily per-
suaded to amend the Constitution, we would be a very
different country today. We would, for instance, have a
President who served for life. Decisions of the Supreme
Court could be overruled by popular vote. Ministers of the
gospel would be prohibited from holding public office. The
President could veto state laws. In fact, states would have
been abolished and the Republic divided into four bureau-
cratic "districts," ruled from Washington. These changes

were incorporated in amendments that were proposed and campaigned for by minority cliques in the past.

Some 4,250 attempts have been made to change the Constitution. Many of them were bitterly disputed by past generations of citizens. Looking back on the proposals now, some seem suicidal and many just plain silly. But, at the time, they all attracted aggressive missionaries and spokesmen.

The wisdom of the early American statesmen who sought a foolproof formula to guarantee a growing nation liberty and prosperity is evident today in the fact that—in all 163 years—only eleven actual amendments have been ratified. Twenty-one amendments have been added to the original 1787 text, but ten were part of the Bill of Rights proposed by the First Congress and are generally considered to be an integral part of the original Constitution. Of the eleven Amendments adopted, most of them gave *more* freedom, *more* rights, and *more* responsibilities to the American people.*

Realizing that no human document could be perfect, the framers of the Constitution included in the text itself provisions for amending it. But they wisely created a procedure so deliberate that no amendment could be put over by a small, organized group or rushed through on a wave of popular sentiment.

Article V prescribes the two methods of amendment. If two-thirds of the members of both houses of Congress

---

* Since this article was written, the Twenty-second Amendment, limiting the office of President to two terms for any one person, has been added to the Constitution.

consider it necessary, the Congress may take the initiative. Should legislatures of two-thirds of the states request it, Congress calls a Constitutional Convention to propose the amendment. But in either case, ratification by legislatures or special conventions of three-fourths of the states must be obtained before the amendment becomes part of the Constitution. This is a nation of *united* states, and the people of three-fourths of them—large or small, rich or poor —have the right to ratify the proposal before it becomes law.

Under the Constitution, the Supreme Court is the official guardian and interpreter of the document. Had the Constitution not contained within itself provision for such a supreme authority to protect the rights and freedoms it proclaimed, we might today be in no better position than the people of other nations that once boasted fine-sounding constitutions.

We Americans have only to look abroad to see how precious the rights and freedoms guaranteed us by our Constitution are in this unhappy world of 1951. We enjoy freedom of religion, speech, press, and peaceful assembly. We are protected from unreasonable searches and seizures, from excessive bail and fines, from cruel and unusual punishment, and from involuntary servitude.

Under the Constitution we still have the right—now lost to millions of other people—to petition the government for redress of grievances, to writs of habeas corpus (which half the human world no longer enjoys), and to swift and public jury trials where we may confront our accusers and make them prove their charges. And all Americans have an equal voice in electing our public servants: the worker's vote is as powerful as that cast by his boss.

We, the People of the United States, are still free. We have preserved not only the inherited words but the living laws of our Constitution. Just as long as we are vigilant against those who would mislead us into surrendering our national heritage, just that long will we continue to be a free and powerful America.

As Thomas Jefferson said, "When we find our Constitution insufficient to secure the happiness of our people, we set it right." But how rarely have we found it necessary to add an Amendment! Thus, as we protect our Constitution, so will our nation endow us with more power and freedom as individuals. Today, as always in the past, America's Constitution remains the world's most enlightened and magnificent political document.

THE SHIP OF STATE

☆

by Henry W. Longfellow

☆

Sail on, sail on, O Ship of State!
   Sail on, O Union, strong and great!
Humanity with all its fears,
   With all the hopes of future years,
Is hanging breathless on thy fate!

We know what Master laid thy keel,
   What Workmen wrought thy ribs of steel,
Who made each mast, and sail, and rope,
   What anvils rang, what hammers beat,
In what a forge and what a heat
   Were shaped the anchors of thy hope!

Fear not each sudden sound and shock,
   'Tis of the wave, and not the rock;
'Tis but the flapping of the sail,
   And not a rent made by the gale!

In spite of rock and tempest roar,
   In spite of false lights on the shore,
Sail on, nor fear to breast the sea!
   Our hearts, our hopes, are all with thee,
Our hearts, our hopes, our prayers, our tears,
   Our faith, triumphant o'er our fears,
Are all with thee, are all with thee!

PSALM 33

Rejoice in the Lord, O ye righteous: *for* praise is comely for the upright.

Praise the Lord with harp: sing unto him with the psaltery *and* an instrument of ten strings.

Sing unto him a new song; play skillfully with a loud noise.

For the word of the Lord *is* right; and all his works *are done* in truth.

He loveth righteousness and judgment: the earth is full of the goodness of the Lord.

By the word of the Lord were the heavens made; and all the host of them by the breath of his mouth.

He gathereth the waters of the sea together as an heap: he layeth up the depth in storehouses.

Let all the earth fear the Lord: let all the inhabitants of the world stand in awe of him.

For he spake, and it was *done;* he commanded, and it stood fast.

The Lord bringeth the counsel of the heathen to nought: he maketh the devices of the people of none effect.

The counsel of the Lord standeth for ever, the thoughts of his heart to all generations.

Blessed *is* the nation whose God *is* the Lord; *and* the people *whom* he hath chosen for his own inheritance.

The Lord looketh from heaven; he beholdeth all the sons of men.

From the place of his habitation he looketh upon all the inhabitants of the earth.

He fashioneth their hearts alike; he considereth all their works.

There is no king saved by the multitude of an host; a mighty man is not delivered by much strength.

An horse *is* a vain thing for safety: neither shall he deliver *any* by his great strength.

Behold, the eye of the Lord *is* upon them that fear him, upon them that hope in his mercy;

To deliver their soul from death, and to keep them alive in famine.

Our soul waiteth for the Lord: he *is* our help and our shield.

For our heart shall rejoice in him, because we have trusted in his holy name.

Let thy mercy, O Lord, be upon us, according as we hope in thee.

OUR COUNTRY

☆

by John Greenleaf Whittier
Read at Woodstock, Connecticut, July 4, 1883

☆

We give thy natal day to hope,
O Country of our love and prayer!
Thy way is down no fatal slope,
But up to freer sun and air.

Tried as by furnace-fires, and yet
By God's grace only stronger made,
In future tasks before thee set
Thou shalt not lack the old-time aid.

The fathers sleep, but men remain
As wise, as true, and brave as they;
Why count the loss and not the gain?
The best is that we have today.

Whate'er of folly, shame, or crime,
Within thy mighty bounds transpires,
With speed defying space and time,
Comes to us on the accusing wires;

While of thy wealth of noble deeds,
Thy homes of peace, thy votes unsold,
The love that pleads for human needs,
The wrong redressed, but half is told!

We read each felon's chronicle,
His acts, his words, his gallows-mood;
We know the single sinner well
And not the nine and ninety good.

Yet if, on daily scandals fed,
We seem at times to doubt thy worth,
We know thee still, when all is said,
The best and dearest spot on earth.

From the warm Mexic Gulf, or where
Belted with flowers Los Angeles
Basks in the semi-tropic air,
To where Katahdin's cedar trees

Are dwarfed and bent by Northern winds,
Thy plenty's horn is yearly filled;
Along, the rounding century finds
Thy liberal soil by free hands tilled.

A refuge for the wronged and poor,
Thy generous heart has borne the blame
That, with them, through thy open door,
The old world's evil outcasts came.

But, with thy just and equal rule,
And labor's need and breadth of lands,
Free press and rostrum, church and school,
Thy sure, if slow, transforming hands,

Shall mould even them to thy design,
Making a blessing of the ban;
And Freedom's chemistry combine
The alien elements of man.

The power that broke their prison bar
And set the dusky millions free,
And welded in the flame of war
The Union fast to Liberty;

Shall it not deal with other ills,
Redress the red man's grievance, break
The Circean cup which shames and kills,
And Labor full requital make?

Alone to such as fitly bear
Thy civic honors bid them fall?
And call thy daughters forth to share
The rights and duties pledged to all?

Give every child his right of school,
Merge private greed in public good,
And spare a treasury overfull
The tax upon a poor man's food?

No lack was in thy primal stock,
No weakling founders builded here;
Thine were the men of Plymouth Rock,
The Huguenot and Cavalier,

And they whose firm endurance gained
The freedom of the souls of men,
Whose hands, unstained with blood, maintained
The swordless commonwealth of Penn.

And thine shall be the power of all
To do the work which duty bids,
And make the people's council hall
As lasting as the Pyramids!

Well have thy later years made good
Thy brave-said word a century back,
The pledge of human brotherhood,
The equal claim of white and black.

That word still echoes round the world,
And all who hear it turn to thee,
And read upon thy flag unfurled
The prophecies of destiny.

Thy great world-lesson all shall learn,
The nations in thy school shall sit,
Earth's farthest mountain tops shall burn
With watch-fires from thy own uplit.

Great without seeking to be great
By fraud or conquest, rich in gold,
But richer in the large estate
Of virtue which thy children hold,

☆

With peace that comes of purity
And strength to simple justice due,
So runs our loyal dream of thee;
God of our fathers! make it true.

O Land of lands! to thee we give
Our prayers, our hopes, our service free;
For thee thy sons shall nobly live,
And at thy need shall die for thee!

STAR-SPANGLED MESSAGE

☆

by Horace Knowles

☆

Most of the world remembers the historic raising of the American flag on Iwo's Mount Suribachi because of Joe Rosenthal's now-famous photograph. But I remember it for another reason.

I was a member of the Third Marine Division intelligence staff during the first part of the battle for Iwo, and my job was to keep a situation map of the island up to date. We were on shipboard, in reserve, and my information about the struggle ashore came from messages intercepted by our radio.

Among the reports I constantly received were those from an observer in a light plane circling above the battlefield. This observer would report everything of significance, giving the target area on the map and a brief description of what was going on. He would say, for example, "TA (Target Area) 182-L, two of our tanks firing into caves," or "TA 183-H, six of our men crawling along a ridge."

About 10:45 in the morning of February 23, 1945, a radioman handed me a message. "TA 132-P," I read, and automatically searched my map to locate the target area. It was Mount Suribachi. Turning back to finish the message, I read, "One flag—red, white and blue."

☆

NAVY GAL

☆

by Fred H. Bohne

1946

☆

The sailor came down the sun-dappled, elm-lined street at an easy rolling gait that carried him right along. He put one long leg in front of the other as if each step were sheer pleasure, as if for a long time he had been confined in narrow and restricted places.

His white hat bobbed through the splashing sunshine like the staysails of a trim, eager schooner, homeward-bound with a fair and following wind. He carried an oblong, paper-wrapped package under his arm, and his pursed lips whistled a jaunty little tune that sounded, to the little peewee, suspiciously like "Three Blind Mice." She could tell he was different, almost at once.

She was swinging on the garden gate when he first hove into sight, her misdemeanor effectively screened from the house by the friendly old lilac bush behind her. It was a big lilac bush, even the path having to swing around it to reach the front door. The sailor, so big and so happy, reminded her of somebody; she couldn't remember whom, but definitely somebody.

Normally, she was a very good little girl, and remembered all the things Mummy told her. Like not swinging on the gate, and like not blurting out things to strangers. But this sailor looked so familiar, as if she ought to know him even if she didn't . . . and the lilac bush could hide one teeny offense as well as another. "H'lo, sailor," she said in a very formal little voice as he came abreast of her.

The sailor, thus abruptly aroused from his own pleasant thoughts, almost snapped his rigging on a sudden starboard tack, came about close-reefed and hauled to. "Hi, little peanut," he called in a voice like the surf, "what's buzzin'?"

It was an unfortunate opening remark. She stepped down off the gate, stood in the opening, and drew herself up to her full three feet. Her straight yellow hair looked as starched as her fresh blue and white pinafore, and both looked as dignifiedly insulted as her sky-blue eyes. "I'm not," she announced in a voice that left little doubt in the matter, "a little peanut! I am a little *peewee;* that's what my daddy calls me."

"Oh," said the sailor, and he snapped his fingers as if he'd never forgive himself, "that's it, of course! The little peewee. And I bet your daddy's awful proud that he has such a cute little peewee for a little girl."

Women of all ages, even five, are tragically susceptible to flattery, and the little peewee favored him with a tentative smile. She also lowered her voice to a slightly more friendly level. "I guess so," she confessed modestly. "He always sends me a big hug 'n' a kiss. My daddy's a sailor, too." There was nothing modest about this part of her confession; in fact her tone brought the sailor's already bulging chest out another full inch.

"Say," he said, stepping closer, "how do you like that; a Navy gal, eh?"

He squatted down so that their eyes were level, and carefully laid his package beside him on the sidewalk. He clasped his hands loosely, and rocked to and fro on his toes in a most friendly fashion. "Say, do you know what? I've got a little girl too. Not as big as you are, but I've never seen her, and she's sure gonna look cute to me." Sailors are a notoriously clannish bunch; they will stop and fan the breeze with a shipmate on the slightest excuse.

The little peewee was duly impressed. "Has your little girl got one of these, too?" she asked. She tried to show him by pushing her chest forward, but succeeded mainly in protruding her tummy in a very undignified and funny manner. But he didn't laugh.

He hadn't seen it before because the blue of it was so nearly the blue in her pinafore. It was really the tiny white stripe in the center of it that now attracted his eye. His low whistle was laden with genuine admiration: "Whew—the Navy Cross! Say, you really have got yourself a daddy, punkin, haven't you?"

He sprang up and grinned warmly as he threw her a snappy salute, and she beamed all over as she proudly returned it. Then the grin faded slowly from his face, and his arm came down inch by inch, as though it had been suddenly chilled. Gosh, thought the little peewee, staring up at his dizzy height, gosh he's big. I guess he's bigger'n anybody I ever saw. I bet he can even look right over the lilac bush.

And then, suddenly, he was down at her level again and looking at her in the strangest way . . . deep into her eyes, as if he wanted to look right through them.

"Your daddy," he said finally in a voice so low she could hardly hear him, "where is he . . . now?"

"Oh," she answered, trying hard to sound pleased, "he's in a very important place. It's pretty far away, and Mummy says he can't come home for a long while yet. . . ." Her voice quavered ever so slightly at that. "But," she added with quick assurance, "I'll be waiting for him."

"Sure, you will," said the sailor. "Sure you will." Then he looked all around, almost as if he'd lost something. Finally his eyes lit on the package beside him on the sidewalk, and he stared at it as if he were seeing it for the first time. And all of a sudden his arm was around her, and her shoulder was pressed against his chest. Their faces were very close.

"Now, isn't it lucky," he said gaily, "that I first made sure you were the right little girl? Your daddy would never forgive me if I had given it to the wrong little girl."

"What!" she cried. "Do you know my daddy?"

"Do I know——" he looked at her askance. "I should say so! 'Now you take this present and give it to my little peewee,' he said to me. 'And mind, you big dope,' he said, 'don't go giving it to the wrong little girl; remember, I said *peewee*, not peanut.' "

"Ooooh!" she squealed with delight, turning full toward him so that he could feel the jumping of her heart. "Did my daddy say that? And is . . . is that the present?"

"Yep." He picked it up and handed it to her. "With a big hug 'n' a kiss, honey, from your daddy . . ." And he suited his actions to his words. She hugged her present with one arm and threw the other around his neck. No one had ever kissed him like that before.

When the sailor and the little peewee finally broke their clinch, and while each was pretending not to notice that the other was acting like a sissy, he meaningly tapped her present. "Aren't you going to open it?" But she made no move to undo the wrapping. Instead she asked, breathlessly, "When's my daddy coming home?"

"Well," he began slowly, speaking in a low, thoughtful voice, and looking deep into her wide attentive eyes, "you see, it's like your mummy said: not for a long, long time yet." He patted her shoulder encouragingly and added hastily: "Your daddy's got an awfully important job where he is, you know. You see, little peewee, us ordinary guys, well, they could afford to let us go home; they don't need us any more. But the important ones, the big guys, like your daddy, who won the war . . . well, you can see that they couldn't possibly get along without them."

The little peewee hung on every word, her face puckered up with the effort to understand. "They had to keep your daddy there, honey," he finished softly, "so they wouldn't forget something very, very important . . ."

For a little while she leaned against him silently, thinking it all over carefully. "I knew my daddy must have a very important job," she said at last, in a voice that was, after all, quite well under control. "All the other flags in our street have a blue star in them, but Mummy put a gold star in my daddy's flag!"

"I know," he said in a voice like a sigh. "I saw it just now when I looked over the lilac bush. Go ahead, sweet-

☆   *214*

heart, open your present. Just wait till you see what your daddy sent you!"

It was the most beautiful doll the little peewee had ever seen. She hugged it ecstatically and, her eyes brimming with joy, stood in front of the gate and waved and waved to him till he turned a corner and was gone.

THE ESSENCE OF THE AMERICAN STORY

☆

by Lewis Galantière

1951

☆

There is a sound reason why foreigners are likely to mis-judge us, and that is, surprisingly, because we misjudge ourselves. We are so in love with the picture of ourselves as individualists that we forget to see ourselves as we really are—the most active cooperators and "joiners" ever assembled in a civilized society.

Sure, we believe in competition in business and in sports, but that does not prevent us from working together for the good of our community with a will and a persistence that are not clearly visible in many of the other free nations left in the world. If anybody is looking for the chief characteristic of American democracy, he will find it in this passion to serve the community, even more than in our individualism.

The key is that word "community." Europeans know what teamwork is. They will get together on the football field or in their version of Christian Endeavor or the Knights of Columbus, in a trade union or a political party. But few among them take the final step that we take in our cities and townships and counties, joining together —Christians and Jews, Catholics and Protestants, manage-ment and labor, Democrats and Republicans—for the good of all.

What characterizes America is this devotion of its citizens to the community as a whole. This is so much a part of our life that we never give it a thought, never think it worth boasting about. I want to boast about it. And I want to say why it is our strongest armor against totalitarianism, both the Communist and the Fascist kind.

Here is a citizens' organization called the National Municipal League. Its purpose is to encourage the elimination of corruption and inefficiency from city government. Is it Republican or Democratic? On the side of the poor or the rich, of capital or of labor? Is it Catholic, Protestant, Jewish? White or Negro? It is none of these and all of them. At its last annual meeting it praised the radical C.I.O. for a job well done in Philadelphia, the conservative Taxpayers Association for reforms introduced in Poughkeepsie, a local United Workers Organization for the clean-up of Bayonne, the League of Women Voters of Grand Rapids for getting rid of a bad mayor, the City Charter Committee of Cincinnati and the Citizens Committee of Worcester for overcoming boss rule, and other local bodies of private citizens for improvements in Cleveland, Boston, San Antonio, Des Moines.

Here is Miami County, Ohio. When its citizens realized that they had among them backward school children, poorly adjusted youths home from the war, more divorce than was seemly, they did not wait for the Government to "vaccinate the community against worries," as they put it. They held a three-day meeting, founded a County Mental Hygiene Association, set up a board with a paid secretary, assessed one another for dues at two dollars a year, and went to work—they, the citizens themselves, serving the whole community.

When the people of Henderson County, Kentucky, took a square look at the illiteracy, tuberculosis, and other disturbing conditions in their region, they did not write to Washington or sit down and weep. They proceeded to do something about it—something so real that it cost them $13,000,000 in added taxes the first year. Though they are country folk, they are not a penny-pinching peasantry.

Let me end this list with an example of a different kind. I pick up a magazine and see that the back cover is filled by an advertisement of United States Savings Bonds in which the sales talk is made by Bob Hope and Bing Crosby. Those supremely popular entertainers lent their names without charge. The ad was prepared by a permanent group of businessmen and advertising experts, called the Advertising Council, who serve the year round in the public interest—again without charge. It carries a line which reads: "Contributed by this magazine in co-operation with the Magazine Publishers of America"— once more without charge.

The purpose of the advertisement, of course, is not alone to sell bonds but to arrest inflation; yet that is not the point. The point is that we do not leave the care of the community to the Government—not by a long shot. There are things government can do which the individual citizen cannot do. We try—at least our aim is—to limit the action of government to those fields.

There is no stronger safeguard against dictatorship than this. In the first place, where self-government is local, the central power at Washington (or Paris or Moscow or New Delhi) cannot get a stranglehold on the country; no conspiracy at the capital can overpower the whole nation. In the second place, the habit of exercising local responsibility preserves the citizen from slipping into a selfish dependence upon government; it nourishes his spirit of self-reliance and makes him a civic fireman—a fellow who is quick to smell the smoke of governmental encroachment and rush to fight it.

The fact is, the strongest enemy of democracy is not Communism as such, or Fascism as such; it is centralized power, whatever may be the political philosophy preached by that power. When Europeans hear us boast of American individualism, they incline to believe that each American lives selfishly for himself—and the devil take the hindmost. Now this misconception may be partly our own fault. Perhaps instead of individualism we ought to speak of *self-reliance*, because that is what we mean. Americans believe that if a man is honest and fearless and energetic he will somehow be able to take care of himself and his family.

Europeans are greatly mistaken who think of us as a young and immature people without traditions, individualists living each for himself and concerned with material things only. We live under an old and uninterrupted political system; we know our system, we work it ourselves. Because we are men, not angels, we work it imperfectly; but we feel for our Constitution and institutions a reverence which has disappeared, alas, from most nations of the earth. Nobody can show us a dreary blueprint of a robot

☆

society and tell us that his sterile intellectual dream-world is better than the living, breathing thing our fathers bequeathed to us.

This is to my mind the long and the short of the American story. Because we are really self-governing, John Stuart Mill was able to pay this tribute to the American people in 1859: "Let them be left without a government, every body of Americans is able to improvise one, and to carry on this or any other public business with a sufficient amount of intelligence, order, and decision. This is what every free people ought to be; and a people capable of this is certain to be free."

AMERICA

☆

by William Dudley Foulke (1848-1935)

☆

Dear land, how God hath cherished thee!
What varied gifts He gave!
A thousand harbours on the sea
To bid thee ride the wave,
And boundless plains and mighty streams
And mountains stocked with ore,
A bounteous sky, a soil that teems—
What could He give thee more?

One treasure that surpasseth all,
A spirit strong and free
In sturdy sons who at thy call
Will die for liberty!
Prize not too much thy goodly state,
Thy wealth beyond compare;
God keep thee pure as thou art great,
As true as thou art fair.

☆

BIBLE VERSES CHOSEN BY THE PRESIDENTS

The following are the first verses of Bible passages selected by the Presidents to be used at their inaugurations. Since Grant's time, it has been customary for the President to place his hand on the selected passage in an open Bible while taking the Oath of Office.

Ulysses S. Grant: And the spirit of the Lord shall rest upon him, the spirit of wisdom and understanding, the spirit of counsel and might, the spirit of knowledge and the fear of the Lord.—Isa. 11:2.

Rutherford B. Hayes: They compassed about me; yea, they compassed me about; but in the name of the Lord I will destroy them.—Ps. 118:11.

James A. Garfield: The king's heart is in the hand of the Lord, as the rivers of water; He turneth it whithersoever He will.—Prov. 21:1.

Chester A. Arthur: In Thee oh Lord, do I put my trust; let me never be ashamed; deliver me in Thy righteousness.—Ps. 31:1.

Grover Cleveland: Praise ye the Lord, Blessed is the man that feareth the Lord, that delighteth greatly in His commandments.—Ps. 112:1. They shall bear thee up in their hands lest thou dash thy foot against a stone.—Ps. 91:12.

Benjamin Harrison: I will lift up mine eyes unto the hills, from whence cometh my help.—Ps. 121:1.

William McKinley: And Cush begat Nimrod; he began to be mighty upon the earth.—I. Chron. 1:10. He that handleth a matter wisely shall find good: and whoso trusteth in the Lord, happy is he.—Prov. 16:20.

Theodore Roosevelt: But be ye doers of the word, and not hearers only, deceiving your own selves.—James 1:22.

William Howard Taft: Give therefore Thy servant an understanding heart to judge Thy people, that I may discern between good and bad; for who is able to judge this thy so great a people?—I. Kings 3:9.

Woodrow Wilson: And take not the word of truth utterly out of my mouth; for I have hoped in Thy judgments.—Ps. 119:43. God is our refuge and strength, a very present help in trouble.—Ps. 46:1.

Warren G. Harding: What doth the Lord require of thee, but to do justly, and to love mercy, and to walk humbly with thy God?—Mic. 6:8.

Calvin Coolidge: In the beginning was the Word, and the Word was with God, and the Word was God.—John 1:1.

Herbert Hoover: Where there is no vision the people perish; but he that keepeth the law, happy is he.—Prov. 29:18.

Franklin D. Roosevelt: Though I speak with the tongues of men and of angels, and have not love, I am become as sounding brass, or a tinkling cymbal. I. Cor. 13:1.*

Harry S. Truman: Blessed are the poor in spirit: for theirs is the kingdom of heaven.—Matt. 5:39. Thou shalt have no other Gods before me.—Exod. 20:3.

Dwight D. Eisenhower: If my people, which are called by my name, shall humble themselves, and pray, and seek my face, and turn from their wicked ways; then will I hear from Heaven, and forgive their sin, and will heal their land. II. Chron. 7:14. Blessed is the nation whose God is the Lord; and the people whom he hath chosen for his own inheritance.—Ps. 33:12.

* Roosevelt used the same verse for his second inauguration and made no selection for the third and fourth.

HUMAN LIBERTY

☆

by Thomas Jefferson
To the New York Legislature, 1809

☆

[Since we are] sole depositories of the remains of human liberty, our duty to ourselves, to posterity, and to mankind calls on us by every motive which is sacred or honorable, to watch over the safety of our beloved country during the troubles which agitate and convulse the residue of the world.

☆

THE PILGRIM FATHERS

☆

by Leonard Bacon (1802-1881)

☆

O God, beneath Thy guiding hand
Our exiled fathers crossed the sea;
And when they trod the wintry strand,
With prayer and psalm they worshiped Thee.

Thou heard'st, well pleased, the song, the prayer:
Thy blessing came; and still its power
Shall onward through all ages bear
The memory of that holy hour.

Laws, freedom, truth, and faith in God
Came with those exiles o'er the waves;
And where their pilgrim feet have trod,
The God they trusted guards their graves.

And here Thy name, O God of love,
Their children's children shall adore,
Till these eternal hills remove,
And spring adorns the earth no more.

HE WAS EVERYBODY GROWN A LITTLE TALLER

☆

John Hancock Mutual Life Insurance Company

1952, 1959

☆

Let's skip all the things you've read about him, all the things you've heard too often or too young. Forget the face on the penny, the speech at Gettysburg. Forget the official things and look at the big thing. What was there about Abraham Lincoln?

He came out of nowhere special. His folks were nobody special. Abe was a smart boy, but not too smart. He told funny stories. He was strong and kind. He'd never try to hurt you, or cheat you, or fool you.

Young Abe worked at odd jobs and read law books at night. Eventually he found his way into local politics. And it was then that people began to know there was something special about Abe Lincoln.

Abe had a habit of growing without changing. So it seemed perfectly natural to find him padding around the White House in his slippers, putting his feet on a chair when he had a deep one to think about. And when the war came that might have torn his country apart, no one doubted what Abe would do. He was a family man. He resolved to keep the American family together.

Abe Lincoln always did what most people would have done, said what they wanted said, thought what they would have thought when they stopped to think about it. He was everybody, grown a little taller—proof of our American faith that greatness comes out of everywhere when it is free to come.

FAREWELL ADDRESS, SPRINGFIELD, ILLINOIS

☆

by *Abraham Lincoln*
February 11, 1861

☆

My friends, no one not in my situation can appreciate my feeling of sadness at this parting. To this place, and the kindness of these people, I owe everything. Here I have lived a quarter of a century, and have passed from a young to an old man. Here my children have been born, and one is buried.

I now leave, not knowing when or whether ever I may return, with a task before me greater than that which rested upon Washington. Without the assistance of that Divine Being who ever attended him I cannot succeed. With that assistance I cannot fail.

Trusting in Him, who can go with me and remain with you, and be everywhere for good, let us confidently hope that all will yet be well. To His care commending you, as I hope in your prayers you will commend me, I bid you an affectionate farewell.

☆

☆

by Abraham Lincoln

November 19, 1863

☆

Fourscore and seven years ago our fathers brought forth on this continent a new nation, conceived in liberty, and dedicated to the proposition that all men are created equal.

Now we are engaged in a great civil war, testing whether that nation, or any nation so conceived and so dedicated, can long endure. We are met on a great battle-field of that war. We have come to dedicate a portion of that field as a final resting-place for those who here gave their lives that that nation might live. It is altogether fitting and proper that we should do this.

But in a larger sense we cannot dedicate, we cannot consecrate, we cannot hallow this ground. The brave men, living and dead, who struggled here have consecrated it, far above our poor power to add or detract. The world will little note nor long remember what we say here, but it can never forget what they did here. It is for us, the living, rather, to be dedicated here to the unfinished work which they who fought here have thus far so nobly advanced. It is rather for us to be here dedicated to the great task remaining before us—that from these honored dead we take increased devotion to that cause for which they gave the last full measure of devotion; that we here highly resolve that these dead shall not have died in vain; that this nation, under God, shall have a new birth of freedom; and that government of the people, by the people, and for the people, shall not perish from the earth.

LETTER TO A GOLD-STAR MOTHER

☆

Executive Mansion
Washington, Nov. 21, 1864

To Mrs. Bixby, Boston, Mass.

Dear Madam—

I have been shown in the files of the War Department a statement of the Adjutant General of Massachusetts that you are the mother of five sons who have died gloriously on the field of battle. I feel how weak and fruitless must be any word of mine which should attempt to beguile you from the grief of a loss so overwhelming. But I cannot refrain from tendering you the consolation that may be found in the thanks of the republic they died to save.

I pray that our Heavenly Father may assuage the anguish of your bereavement, and leave you only the cherished memory of the loved and lost, and the solemn pride that must be yours to have laid so costly a sacrifice upon the altar of freedom.

Yours very sincerely and respectfully,

A. Lincoln

FAITH IN THE RIGHT

☆

by *Abraham Lincoln*

From an address at Cooper Union, New York City,
February 27, 1860

☆

Let us have faith that Right makes Might, and in that faith let us to the end dare to do our duty as we understand it.

HATS OFF TODAY

☆

Daily Courant, *Hartford, Connecticut*
May 30, 1894

☆

Heroism has been truly said to be homely work in the doing. It is good and comforting to remember, on this day of memories, and to never forget that heroic work is mostly done by homely men, by men who are not rich, or famous, or great. The heroes of the Union were, in the phrase of Lincoln, of the plain people, as he was himself, the greatest of them all. They began their education in the common school, and frequently finished it there.

They were laborers and wayfarers like their fathers and like ourselves. They worked in the fields, in factories, in offices, and shops, for self-respect and for the respect of others, and for wives, children, and friends. They were glad at the weddings and sorry at the funerals of their neighborhoods. They had, and showed, a personal interest in politics, local and general. They went to town meetings and caucuses; voted at elections, and stood by their candidates, in victory and in defeat, as later they stood by their guns. They were not perfect; all had their faults, and some the vices of their race and time. They had their private ambitions and disappointments, temptations and triumphs, like every man since Adam. And for joy or grief, and mostly in secret, of course, after the manner of men, they cried sometimes; how else could they have been heroes? A man who is never good for a cry is not good for a fight; his feelings cannot rise to the occasion and stay there. Mere intellect or mere courage, or both together, never made a real man, much less a hero. Heroism is of the heart and so wins all hearts. It is tender with the love and dewy with the tears of all mankind. And so it was that our heroes loved their babies and their country and were ready to fight for both at the first flicker of a hostile flag.

Their work was homely in the doing; none but themselves could know how homely. It was homesickness, weariness and dirt, disease and death, from year's end to year's end. But for their cause, and their heroism in it, there was no debasing work. In that cause and with their devotion to it, their work was the chief glory of their country and century. Year by year, on land and sea, by night and day, through heat and winter wind, scourged by life and racked by death, they fought their starry way to happy peace.

And they builded better than they knew. Heroes always do that. They lived by faith, not by knowledge; and no man's faith was ever yet big enough to divine a hero's estate. Sometimes they die in the mid-stress of their endeavor, knowing nothing of its results; sometimes they live to know a little of the reward of their sacrifices; but, however long they stay, they finally go hence, half knowing and half known, leaving an unclaimed heritage to unborn heirs.

The world does not pay its debt to its benefactors themselves, partly because it is not payable in material things, partly because only the slow ages can at all compute it, and partly because it is not altogether payable by mortals. These continents are not all the world, nor their living inhabitants all its people. Sadly doubting, as men may, of the undiscovered country, they nevertheless cannot doubt of the millions who forelived them, or think in their hearts that those millions are no more. From those millions come earth's heroes, and to them, at last, return. What a welcome theirs must be! Perhaps one who remembers the return of our regiments in 1865 may guess something about it, but it can be quite revealed only to those who go home on their shields. This is the way in which so many of our boys went home a generation ago, and in that way, also, have gone many of their survivors. What a tear-blurred list those names would make today.

And, of all those names, none could be dearer than that of Captain Valentine B. Chamberlain. One year ago next month he died. Many of his comrades, with a multitude of his friends and neighbors, gathered around him in his funeral services. They saw and shared the griefs of the people, to whom he had come in his youth, a citizen soldier, and among whom he lived, as he died, a soldier citizen. They went with him to his final resting place, and, standing there, saw, near and far, around his grave, green mounds glorified by the flag he had followed over the parapet of Wagner, as though his comrades long at rest had roused to give him welcome. And into that gallant company, in the soft brightness of that June afternoon, with the sorrowing eyes of hundreds fixed upon him he disappeared forever. The flags that followed him there were sad with crape; but the flags that paved his coming were glad with sunlight. The comrades who stayed with him to the end turned homeward with the sunlit flags awave in their hearts, like Chamberlain's good-by to his friends and God-speed to his country. Happy in the number as in the character of his children, he will long survive in their loving memory, and will be born to honor and gratitude again and again, in the multiplying generations of his descendants.

How measureless the inheritance which our heroes leave to their children. They may add to their patrimony houses and lands and all the winged riches which fortune gives to labor; and all these things they may lose. They can but keep while life remains one thing which moth and rust cannot corrupt or thieves break through and steal —the priceless treasure of heroic blood. A man with Gettysburg in his veins is richer than the Indies, though the Indies drained the wealth of all the zones. Emerson was right:

A ruddy drop of manly blood
The surging sea outweighs.

Our old soldiers know the truth. They have seen it in the service of heavy fights and the valley of the shadow of death. They have felt it in all the personal reverses and civil turmoils of these last thirty years and they feel it more and more, as in faded blue, they face their fading west.

Hats off today, for the war of the Union marches past! Hats off to its old men and its old flag! Hats off to its flag lit by new flame, to its men, now forever young, who fell at the front or died at their homes! Hats off to Liberty, sweet Mother of us all, who mourns among our dead her sons of many lands!

. . . .

Now that the battle roar dies away in the distance, what choral harmonies flood in from thirty years ago—pipes of the Scottish border, sounds of the English lanes, strains of the "Marseillaise," songs of the Fatherland, chants of the Emerald Isle, and, rising above all, like a soul set free, the roll of Appomattox drums chanting for the ages our litany of the knights.

THE BLUE AND THE GRAY

☆

by Francis Miles Finch (*1827-1907*)

Lawyer, judge, lecturer
Atlantic Monthly, *1867*

☆

By the flow of the inland river,
Whence the fleets of iron have fled,
Where the blades of grave grass quiver,
Asleep are the ranks of the dead;
Under the sod and the dew,
Waiting the judgment day—
Under the one, the blue;
Under the other, the gray.

These in the robings of glory,
Those in the gloom of defeat,
All, with the battle blood gory,
In the dusk of eternity meet;
Under the sod and the dew,
Waiting the judgment day—
Under the laurel, the blue;
Under the willow, the gray.

From the silence of sorrowful hours
The desolate mourners go,
Lovingly laden with flowers
Alike for the friend and the foe;
Under the sod and the dew,

Waiting the judgment day—
Under the roses, the blue;
Under the lilies, the gray.

So with an equal splendor
The morning sun-rays fall,
With a touch impartially tender,
On the blossoms blooming for all;
Under the sod and the dew,
Waiting the judgment day—
'Broidered with gold, the blue;
Mellowed with gold, the gray.

So, when the summer calleth
On forest and field of grain,
With an equal murmur falleth
The cooling drip of the rain;
Under the sod and the dew,
Waiting the judgment day—
Wet with rain, the blue;
Wet with rain, the gray.

Sadly, but not with upbraiding,
The generous deed was done;
In the storm of the years that are fading,
No braver battle was won;
Under the sod and the dew,
Waiting the judgment day—
Under the blossoms, the blue;
Under the garlands, the gray.

No more shall the war-cry sever,
Or the winding rivers be red;
They banish our anger forever
When they laurel the graves of our dead!
Under the sod and the dew,
Waiting the judgment day—
Love and tears for the blue;
Tears and love for the gray.

Atlantic Monthly, 1867

☆

PRAYER FOR AMERICA

☆

Anonymous

☆

Oh, God on high, we pray to Thee:
Preserve this land of liberty,
The land where heroes fought and died
To stem oppression's rising tide,
The only land upon the earth
Where all may rise above their birth,

Whose people seek to keep these shores
Immune from class and racial wars,
Whose Eagle's not a bird of prey,
But one who guards us night and day.
Protect us from dissension's hates—
Lord bless our great United States.

UNMANIFEST DESTINY

☆

by Richard Hovey (*1864-1900*)

1898

☆

To what new fates, my country, far
And unforeseen of foe or friend,
Beneath what unexpected star,
Compelled to what unchosen end?

Across the sea that knows no beach
The Admiral of Nations guides
Thy blind obedient keels to each
The harbor where thy future rides!

The guns that spoke at Lexington
Knew not that God was planning then
The trumpet word of Jefferson
To bugle forth the rights of men.

To them that wept and cursed Bull Run,
What was it but despair and shame?
Who saw behind the cloud the sun?
Who knew that God was in the flame?

Had not defeat upon defeat,
Disaster on disaster come,

The slave's emancipated feet
Had never marched behind the drum.

There is a Hand that bends our deeds
To mightier issues than we planned,
Each son that triumphs, each that bleeds,
My country, serves Its dark command.

I do not know beneath what sky
Nor on what seas shall be thy fate;
I only know it shall be high,
I only know it shall be great.

SENATE PRAYER

☆

by *Peter Marshall*

June 3, 1948

(During April, May, and June in Washington there is a constant procession of buses filled with American high school students. Most of them visit the Senate to see it in action.)

☆

Our Father in Heaven, as we pray for Thy blessings upon the Members of the Senate, we are not unmindful of those in the gallery who join us in this prayer.

We give Thee thanks for the youth of America, the leaders of tomorrow, the young people who shall some day take our places. We thank Thee for their faith in America, and we pray that nothing done or said in this place shall cause them to think any less of the institutions we cherish.

Challenge them, we pray Thee, with the vision of good citizenship and a love for all that is good in America and a desire to make it even better, that this land that we love may become in truth and in fact God's own country. Amen.

☆

THEY SEE A VISION THAT ONCE WAS YOURS

☆

John Hancock Mutual Life Insurance Company
1952, 1960

☆

You may remember how it was.

You sat in the wide-eyed silence that fire and the night bring, and stared into the flames, and you felt like a very special boy.

Not long before, you'd been an ordinary boy. Then, one day, you stood up before a lot of envious grown-ups and made a Promise. "On my honor, I will do my best to do my duty to God and my country, and to obey the Scout Law; to help other people at all times; to keep myself physically strong, mentally awake, and morally straight."

You said that—and suddenly you were special. You were trustworthy, loyal, helpful, friendly, and too excited to sleep. You were courteous, kind, obedient, cheerful, and mighty proud of yourself. You were thrifty, brave, clean, reverent, and twice the boy you were before.

They could drop you in the desert now, and you'd find water. They could lose you at the North Pole, and you'd make a warm bed in the snow. You could tie a square knot, bandage an ankle, cook dandelion soup, drum out a message on a hollow log, and say *quawk-quawk* like a heron. You were ready for anything. You were a Scout.

The world changed for the better, too. It became full of forest fires waiting for you to put them out, full of ladies with packages needing to be helped across the street. Your country's history moved in to live with you. You could hear prairie schooners on Main Street. When you sat by the campfire, Daniel Boone was there, and the rest of the pioneers. You knew now what made those fellows tick. They were scouts, too.

Eventually, you grew older. And you had to admit that maybe you couldn't always find the right trail; maybe you couldn't always put out the forest fire single-handed; maybe you weren't always as helpful, as courteous, as cheerful, as brave, as you wanted to be. But a lot of the time you were. Some of it had stuck. A bit of the boy you thought you were, as you sat dreaming into the fire, had found its way into the man you are today.

The future of any country starts with the pictures that pass through a boy's mind. In America tonight, a couple of million kids are trying hard to be good scouts . . . thinking up a couple of million good turns.

☆

MAGIC MOMENT

☆

by Conrad C. Lautenbacher, Jr.

This selection won the Best Editorial Award in the Boys' Life *Writing Contest and was published in the magazine's All-Boy Issue of May, 1959. The author was a sixteen-year-old senior at Central High School, Philadelphia, an Eagle Scout, Junior Assistant Scoutmaster, member of the school orchestra, varsity swimmer and soccer player. In January, 1960, upon graduation, he received an appointment to the United States Naval Academy at Annapolis.*

☆

The rhythmic cadence of marching feet re-echoed from hill to hill as the sun's last visible rays faded into the back-log of eternity. The sound was not the ominous tread of a forced movement somewhere behind the Iron Curtain, but the happy, youthful step of liberty on the march. At first, the sound seemed remote, significant only in the fact that it was noise—noise that would grow deeper and broader until it encompassed 52,000 pairs of marching feet, 52,000 voices. As the volume increased, the marchers themselves became cognizant of the sound, until they were swept away by the almost joyous solemnity of the occasion.

Like the spokes of a gigantic wheel from the rim of the horizon, the columns of twos converged on a natural amphitheater, representing the hub. Nearing their goal, the marchers changed the pattern into a huge semi-circle, as the 52,000 similarly-clad boys seated themselves on the hillside's gentle slope to take part in the closing ceremonies of the Fourth National Jamboree, at Valley Forge, Pennsylvania. From every corner of America and many foreign countries, Scouts of all faiths, creeds, and colors intermingled.

Before them, outlined against the deep purple background of night, by an amazing system of foot and overhead lights, was an improvised stage the size of a football field. In the center of the platform, and dominating the scene, a huge round painting of George Washington, kneeling in prayer, carried out the theme of the jamboree, "Onward for God and My Country." Above the picture, Old Glory furled and unfurled in the breeze.

The long walk from the campsite had seemed short because each participant was thinking not alone of the previous ten days spent in fellowship and fun, but of the winter of 1777-1778, one hundred and eighty years ago. Recalling those early days of the republic made each boy proud of his heritage and grateful for the opportunity to camp on the hallowed spot where Washington and his gallant army of brave patriots had held out, starving and ragged, against wintry blasts.

The stage lights were slowly extinguished until the sky, which resembled a gigantic canopy of black velvet studded with brilliants, provided the only illumination. The long-awaited moment had come for each boy to light the candle he had brought with him from his campsite. There was the signal!

Suddenly the dark hillside burst into blooms of tiny, flickering flames! To some, the panorama presented a sea of small suns; to others, a lake of Lilliputian lanterns. From the participants came gasps of delight at the beauty of the scene. The picture was indelibly photographed forever in the memory of each boy. And then the clear, inspired voice of Scout Dick Chappell, coming from the South Pole via ham radio, began the Scout Oath. Solemnly and reverently, 52,000 voices joined in.

These were magic moments—moments that come but once in a lifetime.

OUR HERITAGE

To the Boy Scouts of America

☆

by Bernard Baruch

November, 1955

☆

This land is your heritage. It offers you freedom, opportunity, well-being. Its Constitution and its institutions represent the finest work that man, with all his experiments in government, has yet devised. Always the haven of the oppressed, the island of hope in the sea of fear, it is today the last fortress of freedom in the whole world. Guard it well, not only from the dark forces which menace us from afar, but from the weakness, selfishness, and disunity that threatens us near at hand.

If you, the trustees of posterity, the hope of the future, carry out in letter and in spirit your Scout Oath, we will have peace and the better life to which America is dedicated.

☆

MANKIND'S SACRED RIGHTS

☆

by Alexander Hamilton

From a letter to a Westchester farmer, February 5, 1775

☆

The Sacred Rights of Mankind are not to be rummaged for among old parchments or musty records. They are written, as with a sunbeam, in the whole volume of human nature, by the Hand of the Divinity itself, and can never be erased or obscured by mortal power.

FAITH OF OUR FATHERS!

☆

by Frederick W. Faber (1814-63)

☆

Faith of our fathers! living still
In spite of dungeon, fire and sword:
O how our hearts beat high with joy,
Whene'er we hear that glorious word:
Faith of our fathers, holy faith!
We will be true to thee till death.

Our fathers, chained in prisons dark,
Were still in heart and conscience free:
How sweet would be their children's fate,
If they, like them, could die for thee!
Faith of our fathers, holy faith!
We will be true to thee till death.

Faith of our fathers! faith and prayer
Shall keep our country true to thee;
And through the truth that comes from **God,**
Our land shall then indeed be free.
Faith of our fathers, holy faith!
We will be true to thee till death.

Faith of our fathers! we will love
Both friend and foe in all our strife:

And preach thee, too, as love knows how,
By kindly deeds and virtuous life.
Faith of our fathers, holy faith!
We will be true to thee till death.

"AMERICA, IT'S MAGNIFIQUE, MOMMY!"

☆

by Jean Potter

1956

Young Michael was scared, a stranger in his own country.
Then he discovered the heart of his homeland.

☆

"But I don't want to go to America!" my seven-year-old son Michael angrily told me, in French.

"It's your country," I reminded him. "You've never seen it, but I'm sure you're going to love it there."

He stood beside me in our Paris apartment as I packed the trunks, a small, stormy figure in short pants and school smock, most unimpressed.

When my husband and I returned home after an eight-year assignment abroad we knew, of course, that our son would not welcome the change. Michael had been born in Europe and grown up happily in Paris. But we were surprised by the force of his reluctance to leave.

"American boys are rough and rude," he told me. "They're dumb and mean and they fight all the time. America is full of machines and gangsters. The only good thing is cowboys."

I asked him where he had heard such nonsense.

"Oh, it's all true," he said, with the loftiness of seven years. "The boys told me at school."

For the first time I realized how very European our child was. He'd attended a French school—in the stern tradition of the Continent—each day from nine to five. He did not even speak English.

In the formal little Paris park where he spent his play time, weekends and holidays, the children were not allowed to walk on the grass. His playmates were polite small fry who seldom shouted or got their *chic* clothes dirty. They were always accompanied by mothers or nursemaids. One little *monsieur* even wore white gloves.

On the boat trip to New York we tried to give Michael a tardy coaching in English. But he stubbornly declined to cooperate. When we arrived at the town of Carmel, California, where we were to live for four months, he cried bitterly at the prospect of going to school.

It was then that I called on Mrs. Marjorie McCausland, principal of the neighborhood public school, to prepare her for my "un-American" American son. I apologized politely, as one does in Paris, for "bothering" her.

A warm, vivacious woman, she listened carefully to my story and said with a smile, "But we're *happy* to have Michael. We'll consider it a challenge."

I was startled. I had forgotten how friendly and out-going Americans are.

I explained that I was anxious about how Michael would get along with the other children.

"The children?" She leaned across her desk, cheerful and emphatic. "But it's the children I'm counting on to help him the most."

She outlined her plan for easing Michael's adjustment. She would have the teachers explain his problem to their pupils before he arrived. And she would assign boys of his age to guide him around, the first week—a different one each day.

"We'll make it a kind of rotating honor," she told me.

I was astonished. A public school take such pains to make a misfit feel welcome?

It was a very scared little boy in brand-new blue jeans, T-shirt, and sneakers that I delivered to her office two days later. He was saying nothing. But he seemed determined to keep up a front. He pumped her outstretched hand briskly and stiffly, in the best French schoolboy manner.

"This is Tim, Michael," she told him, very slowly.

A lanky little redhead stepped forward.

"Tim is going to show you around today, and he'll stay with you all the time." She spoke gaily, as if it were a party. "Tim, show Michael where to put his lunchbox, on the shelf beside yours."

Michael was eying Tim warily.

"Okay?" asked Tim, very affable. He touched Michael's arm gently, leading him to the door.

The hours dragged for me till I could pick Michael up at two.

The yard was almost empty when I saw him. He was coming at a fast run with Tim and two other boys. His face was flushed, his hair tousled. He was laughing.

"We were showing him how to play kick," one of his escorts told me. "He's catching on."

" 'Bye, Mike!" they called as we started away.

Michael seemed dazed. "This school is different," he volunteered. He said little more.

The next morning, as we were walking toward the school, a boy came running out of a house.

"Hi, Mike!" he shouted, smiling.

Michael started as to a rifle shot. Then, as he recognized the child, he smiled back, shyly, but as if they shared some remarkable secret.

"You don't have to take him to school," the boy told me. "He can walk with me."

Michael did not hesitate.

A week later, he came home bursting with excitement.

"I'm class president!" he announced.

He laughed, both proud and sheepish.

"I didn't know what they were doing, writing on all those slips of paper. I thought it was a game. Then they all started looking at me and clapping. I didn't understand till a man came who spoke some French. He told me I was president."

A shadow crossed his face.

"The only trouble," he said, "is that he didn't tell me what I'm supposed to do."

Certain that he must be having delusions of grandeur, I called his teacher that evening. She assured me that Michael was president for the month. "What a time we had explaining it to him," she laughed. "Luckily our janitor speaks some French and I could send for him."

"Was this *your* idea?" I asked, dumbfounded.

"Oh, no!" she seemed shocked. "I never have anything to do with the children's choice."

I was too overcome for a moment to say anything else to her.

"He seems rather at sea about his duties," I finally managed.

"Oh, *they* know that," she said. "The vice-president will sit next to Michael and pinch-hit. He'll enjoy coaching him."

Only once did Michael satisfy our burning curiosity about his progress in office.

"I hold the flag in the mornings," he proudly told us. Although he was still declining to speak English at home, he was, we learned, trying a lot of it at school.

In the month that followed, Michael became extremely surly and difficult. The teacher confirmed our suspicion that things were going less smoothly. No longer treated as a distinguished foreign visitor, he was trying to find himself as just another American boy.

Then, unexpectedly, came the trouble that I had feared. Michael told me one morning that he could not go to school; he had "a terrible cold." As he had no sign of a cold, we sent him off, crying. Later, I called his teacher.

"Yes," she told me, "something did happen. But it's all right now."

She'd learned that some of the boys had been hazing him at the playground, calling him a "silly French kid." She had put the matter before the class that morning, without mentioning names, and asked if those who knew about the trouble at the playground wanted to talk it out now. Or settle it later.

They had voted for the second course. During the recess there had been huddles, while Michael stood awkwardly apart. Then one of the ringleaders sidled over to him and apologized.

"That's not all," she told me. "When we convened again, Michael raised his hand. It's the first time he's ever asked to speak in class. He spoke loud and clearly. He seemed determined to make himself understood. He said, 'Some boy tell me he's sorry. I think and think but I don't know why he's sorry. I don't remember.'

"It struck me as high diplomacy," she said, proud and pleased. "The children, and Michael himself, have cleared the matter up—and with no hard feelings left over."

Michael was eager to go to school after that. He made marked progress with his lessons and his disposition at home changed from storm to sunshine.

One day a copy of his old school paper arrived from Paris. Remembering how avidly he used to read it, I handed it to him. He glanced at it vaguely and put it down.

"I'm going outdoors," he said.

American parents cannot appreciate what "going outdoors" means to a child who has been raised abroad. The freedom of roaming unchaperoned through yards without any walls around them is a new-found heaven.

"America, it's *magnifique*, Mommy!" Michael told me one day, his eyes shining.

He was now speaking with us half in French, half in English. If his languages were mixed, his feelings were not. He was radiantly happy.

Coached by his small colleagues, he was becoming an American boy with dramatic speed. I was impressed by their tact. They only corrected him when a mistake was extreme.

"Not sheep, Mike. That's an animal. Ship."

"Oh, no!" he shouted, doubling up with clownish laughter. "Not an *animal!*" Somehow he had learned to make fun of his own mistakes, perhaps because the others were laughing too—not at him, with him.

The day I fully realized how little Michael's principal, teacher, and classmates had let him feel like a foreign misfit was the day we left Carmel for the East.

"How *can* I leave my friends?" he asked, tears in his eyes. "They're the first *real* friends I ever had. I'll never find such friends again!"

He'd known them only four months, yet he minded leaving them much more than he'd minded leaving the children he'd grown up with in Paris for many years.

His classmates gave him a baseball as a going-away present. They'd printed their names on it with ink, and the year. He was carrying the ball in his hand as we boarded a plane for New York. He'd refused to put it in a suitcase.

Today, in New Jersey, he is happy with a new group of "American gangster" boys. But he's not playing with the baseball his "first real friends" gave him. One day I found him carefully sticking scotch tape over their names.

"I don't want the ink to rub off," he explained, and laid it gently on a shelf. "I'll need another ball to play with."

He stood silent a moment, very grave.

"You see," he confided, "this ball—it's sort of the way

your diamond ring is to you, Mommy. I always want to keep it."

I understood. What he had received was precious.

I was more than grateful. I had glimpsed through my "French" son's wondering eyes a vision of America, of its free and friendly democratic spirit, that I had not seen as clearly before.

INAUGURAL ADDRESS

☆

by Dwight D. Eisenhower

From a speech delivered at Columbia University, October 12, 1948

☆

The common responsibility of all Americans is to become effective, helpful participants in a way of life that blends and harmonizes the fiercely competitive demands of the individual and of society. The individual must be free, able to develop to the utmost of his ability, employing all opportunities that confront him for his own and his family's welfare; otherwise he is merely a cog in a machine. The society must be stable, assured against violent upheaval and revolution; otherwise it is nothing but a temporary truce with chaos. But freedom for the individual must never degenerate into the brutish struggle for survival that we call barbarism. Neither must the stability of society ever degenerate into the enchained servitude of the masses that we call statism.

Only when each individual, while seeking to develop his own talents and further his own good, at the same time protects his fellows against injury and cooperates with them for the common betterment—only then is the fullness of orderly, civilized life possible to the millions of men who live within a free nation.

The citizenship which enables us to enjoy this fullness is our most priceless heritage. By our possession and wise use of it we enjoy freedom of body, intellect, and spirit, and in addition material richness beyond the boast of Babylon. To insure its perpetuation and proper use is the first function of our educational system.

To blend, without coercion, the individual good and the common good is the essence of citizenship in a free country. This is truly an art whose principles must be learned. . . . . .

Democratic citizenship is concerned with the sum total of human relations. Here at home this includes the recognition of mutual dependence for liberty, livelihood and existence of more than one hundred forty million human beings. Moreover, since we cannot isolate ourselves as a nation from the world, citizenship must be concerned too with the ceaseless impact of the globe's two billion humans upon one another, manifested in all the multitudinous acts and hopes and fears of humanity.

The educational system, therefore, can scarcely impose any logical limit upon its functions and responsibilities in preparing students for a life of social usefulness and individual satisfaction. The academic range must involve the entire material, intellectual, and spiritual aspects of life.

Underlying this structure of knowledge and understanding is one immutable, incontestable fact: Time and again, over the span of the last 700 years it has been proved that those who know our way of life place upon one thing greater value than upon any other—and that priceless thing is individual liberty. This requires a system of self-government which recognizes that every person possesses certain inalienable rights and that rules and regulation for the common good may be imposed only by the ultimate authority of the citizens themselves.

This individual freedom is not the product of accident. To gain and retain it our forefathers have sacrificed material wealth, have undergone suffering, indeed have given life itself. So it is with us today.

But it is not enough merely to realize how freedom has been won. Essential also is it that we be ever alert to all threats to that freedom. Easy to recognize is the threat from without. Easy too is it to see the threat of those who advocate its destruction from within. Less easy is it to see the dangers that arise from our own failure to analyze and understand the implications of various economic, social and political movements among ourselves.

Thus, one danger arises from too great a concentration of power in the hands of any individual or group: The power of concentrated finance, the power of selfish pressure groups, the power of any class organized in opposition to the whole—any one of these, when allowed to dominate, is fully capable of destroying individual freedom as is power concentrated in the political head of the state.

The concentration of too much power in centralized government need not be the result of violent revolution or great upheaval. A paternalistic government can gradually destroy, by suffocation in the immediate advantage of subsidy, the will of a people to maintain a high degree of individual responsibility. And the abdication of individual responsibility is inevitably followed by further concentration of power in the state. Governmental ownership or control of property is not to be decried principally because of the historic inefficiency of government management of productive enterprises; its real threat rests in the fact that, if carried to the logical extreme, the final concentration of ownership in the hands of government gives to it, in all practical effects, absolute power over our lives.

There are internal dangers that require eternal vigilance if they are to be avoided. If we permit extremes of wealth for a few and enduring poverty for many, we shall create social explosiveness and a demand for revolutionary change. If we do not eliminate selfish abuse of power by any one group, we can be certain that equally selfish retaliation by other groups will ensue. Never must we forget that ready cooperation in the solution of human problems is the only sure way to avoid forced government intervention.

All our cherished rights—the right of free speech, free worship, ownership of property, equality before the law—all these are mutually dependent for their existence. Thus, when shallow critics denounce the profit motive inherent in our system of private enterprise, they ignore the fact that it is an economic support of every human right we possess and that without it, all rights would soon disappear. Demagoguery, unless combatted by truth, can become as great a danger to freedom as exists in any other threat.

It was loss of unity through demagogic appeals to class selfishness, greed, and hate that Macaulay, the English historian, feared would lead to the extinction of our democratic form of government. More than ninety years ago he wrote of these fears to the American historian, H. S. Randall. In a letter of May 23, 1857 he said, ". . . when a society has entered on this downward progress, either civilization or liberty must perish. Either some

Caesar or Napoleon will seize the reins of government with a strong hand; or your republic will be as fearfully plundered and laid waste by barbarians in the twentieth century as the Roman Empire was in the fifth;—with this difference, that the Huns and Vandals who ravaged the Roman Empire came from without, and that your Huns and Vandals will have been engendered within your own country by your own institutions."

That day shall never come if in our educational system we help our students gain a true understanding of our society, of the need for balance between individual desires and the general welfare, and of the imperative requirement that every citizen participate intelligently and effectively in democratic affairs. The broadest possible citizen understanding and responsibility is as necessary in our complex society as was mere literacy before the industrial revolution.

It follows, then, that every institution built by free men, including great universities, must be first of all concerned with the preservation and further development of human freedom—despite any contrary philosophy or force that may be pitted against it.

At all levels of education, we must be constantly watchful that our schools do not become so engrossed in techniques, great varieties of fractionalized courses, highly specialized knowledge, and the size of their physical plant as to forget the principal purpose of education itself—to prepare the student for an effective personal and social life in a free society. From the school at the crossroads to a university as great as Columbia, general education for citi-

☆

zenship must be the common and first purpose of them all.

I do not suggest less emphasis on pure research or on vocational or professional training; nor am I by any means suggesting that curricula should be reduced to the classical education of the nineteenth century. But I deeply believe that all of us must demand of our schools more emphasis on those fundamentals that make our free society what it is and that assure it boundless increase in the future if we comprehend and apply them.

. . . .

Love of freedom, confidence in cooperative effort, faith in the American way will live so long as our schools loyally devote themselves to truly liberal education. . . . . .

Who among us can doubt the choice of future Americans, as between statism and freedom, if the truth concerning each be constantly held before their eyes? But if we, as adults, attempt to hide from the young the facts in this world struggle, not only will we be making a futile attempt to establish an intellectual "iron curtain," but we will arouse the lively suspicion that statism possesses virtues whose persuasive effect we fear.

The truth is what we need—the full truth. . . . . . Enlightenment is not only a defender of our institutions, it is an aggressive force for the defeat of false ideologies.

America was born in rebellion, and rebellion against wrong and injustice is imbedded in the American temper. But whatever change our rebels of the American past may have sought, they were quick to proclaim it openly and fearlessly, preaching it from the house-tops. We need their sort . . . informed, intelligent rebels against ignorance and imperfection and prejudice. . . . . . because they have sought the truth and know it, they will be loyal to the American way, to the democracy within which we live. . . . . .

The American university does not operate in an unreal world of its own, concerned solely with the abstract, secluded from the worrisome problems of workaday living, insulated against contact with those other institutions which constitute our national structure. Just as the preservation of the American way demands a working partnership among all 146 million Americans, its continued development demands a working partnership between universities and all other free institutions.

The school, for example, that enjoys a partnership with the manufacturing industries and labor unions and mercantile establishments of its community is a better and more productive school in consequence of its non-academic associations. Its influence permeates the entire community and is multiplied many times over while the school itself, energized by the challenges and dynamism of community life, grows and broadens with each problem it helps surmount.

Together, the university and the community—the entire record of human experience at their call, able to apply academic, technical and practical knowledge to the problem, joined in voluntary cooperative effort—together they can analyze and evaluate and plan. By such partnership, it is not too much to hope that the university—losing none of its own freedom, but rather extending its academic horizons—will in time help develop a new freedom for America—freedom from industrial strife.

Partnership is the proof and product of unity. But in a free democracy unity is possible only through intelligent and unswerving adherence to fundamental principles. . . . . .

To build a stouter unity among our people is the most worthy of goals. For a united America is the greatest temporal power yet seen upon the earth—a power dedicated to the betterment and happiness of all mankind.

THE WAY TO GREATNESS

☆

by Herbert Hoover

Spoken at Valley Forge in February, 1931,
and repeated in February, 1958

☆

The nation is beset with difficulties and confusions. Many of us have doubt and grave concern for the future. But no one who reviews the past and realizes the vast strength of our people can doubt that this, like a score of similar experiences in our history, is a passing trial. From this knowledge must come the courage and wisdom to improve and strengthen us for the future.

We must not be misled by the claim that the source of all wisdom is in the Government. Wisdom is born out of experience, and most of all out of precisely such experience as is brought to us by the darkest moments. It is in the meeting of such moments that are born new insights, new sympathies, new powers, new skills.

Such conflicts as we are in the midst of today cannot be won by any single stroke, by any one strategy sprung from the mind of any single genius. Rather must we pin our faith upon the inventiveness, the resourcefulness, the initiative of every one of us. That cannot fail us if we keep faith in ourselves and our future, and in the constant growth of our intelligence and ability to cooperate with one another.

The memory of Americans who glory in Valley Forge

☆

tells us the truth which echoes upward from this soil of blood and tears: *the way to greatness is the path of self-reliance, independence, and steadfastness in time of trial and stress.*

WHAT IS A FOOTBALL PLAYER?

☆

by Charles Loftus, 1951

Director of Sports Information, Yale University

☆

BETWEEN the innocence of boyhood and the dignity of man, we find a sturdy creature called a football player. Football players come in assorted weights, heights, jersey colors, and numbers, but all football players have the same creed: to play every second of every minute of every period of every game to the best of their ability.

FOOTBALL players are found everywhere—underneath, on top of, running around, jumping over, passing by, twisting from or driving through the enemy. Teammates rib them, officials penalize them, students cheer them, kid brothers idolize them, coaches criticize them, college girls adore them, alumni tolerate them, and mothers worry about them. A football player is Courage in cleats, Hope in a helmet, Pride in pads, and the best of Young Manhood in moleskins.

WHEN your team is behind, a football player is incompetent, careless, indecisive, lazy, uncoordinated, and stupid. Just when your team threatens to turn the tide of battle, he misses a block, fumbles the ball, drops a pass, jumps offside, falls down, runs the wrong way, or completely forgets his assignment.

A FOOTBALL player is a composite—he eats like Notre Dame, sleeps like Notre Dame, but, more often than not, plays like Grand Canyon High. To an opponent publicity man, he has the speed of a gazelle, the strength of an ox, the size of an elephant, the cunningness of a fox, the agility of an adagio dancer, the quickness of a cat, and the ability of Red Grange, Glen Davis, Bronco Nagurski, and Jim Thorpe—combined.

TO HIS own coach he has, for press purposes, the stability of mush, the fleetness of a snail, the mentality of a mule, is held together by adhesive tape, bailing wire, sponge rubber, and has about as much chance of playing on Saturday as would his own grandfather.

TO AN ALUMNUS a football player is someone who will never kick as well, run as far, block as viciously, tackle as hard, fight as fiercely, give as little ground, score as many points, or generate nearly the same amount of spirit as did those particular players of his own yesteryear.

A FOOTBALL player likes game films, trips away from home, practice sessions without pads, hot showers, long runs, whirlpool baths, recovered fumbles, points after touchdowns, and the quiet satisfaction which comes from being part of a perfectly executed play. He is not much for wind sprints, sitting on the bench, rainy days, aftergame compliments, ankle wraps, scouting reports, or calisthenics.

NO ONE ELSE looks forward so much to September or so little to December. Nobody gets so much pleasure out of knocking down, hauling out, or just plain bringing down the enemy. Nobody else can cram into one mind assignments for an end run, an off-tackle slant, a jump pass, a quarterback sneak, a dive play, punt protection, kick-off returns, a buck lateral, goal line stands, or a spinner cycle designed to result in a touchdown every time it is tried.

A FOOTBALL player is a wonderful creature—you can criticize him, but you can't discourage him. You can defeat his team, but you can't make him quit. You can get him out of a game, but you can't get him out of football. Might as well admit it—be you alumnus, coach or fan—he is your personal representative on the field, your symbol of fair and hard play. He may not be an All-American, but he is an example of the American way. He is judged, not for his race, not for his religion, not for his social standing, or not for his finances, but by the democratic yardstick of how well he blocks, tackles, and sacrifices individual glory for the over-all success of his teams.

HE IS A HARD-working, untiring, determined kid doing the very best he can for his school or college. And when you come out of a stadium, grousing and feeling upset that your team has lost, he can make you mighty ashamed with just two sincerely spoken words—"We tried!"

HONOR ROLL

☆

by Grace Noll Crowell

1943

☆

They went away, the sunlight in their eyes,
The bright wind blowing through their shining hair:
Our church's youth grown suddenly so wise,
Their chins outthrust, their shoulders straight and square.
The vacancies they left cannot be filled,
A silence reigns down vestibule and hall,
The high exuberance of youth is stilled
In answer to their country's urgent call.

God keep them close within thy loving care;
God help them win their high and glorious goal
Of peace for all mankind—this is our prayer:
Hold close each one upon our Honor Roll,
And here at home may we be brave as they
Who battle for a brighter, better day.

THE REAL STORY OF RODGER YOUNG

☆

by Stanley A. Frankel, 1950

Rodger Young's company commander

☆

There are thousands of smoky coral islands scattered like emeralds across the blue velvet of the Pacific. They are quiet now.

But, hidden by the dank jungle growth of those islands that marched into history a few brief years ago, are countless rusting steel skeletons. There are buckling concrete airstrips, and crumbling buildings that have not quite succumbed to the creeping jungle.

The men who ripped up those islands, hacked out the airfields, and filled the vastness of the Pacific with war, are gone. Even those who fought and died there are gone. They have returned home—along with the living—and the South Pacific is silent once more.

But their deeds can never be silenced. They are written in records and history books, and in the hearts of our people.

The deed of one man who died there is perhaps more widely known than it might have been in the ordinary annals of heroism. He is remembered because of a song.

Most Americans have heard the ballad of Rodger Young, and many know the stirring words. Military bands march to its swinging rhythm. School children sing it at assembly.

Rodger Young died on a little island called New

☆

Georgia. He died in such a way that he was awarded a posthumous Congressional Medal of Honor and was chosen from amongst many heroes to be immortalized in a song of the infantry.

It should be enough to record that Rodger Young died a hero. But the facts show that he proved himself a hero several weeks before the fateful day that won him the nation's highest honor. Yet perhaps only a half dozen of his comrades in battle know the real and complete story of his quiet gallantry.

It began on a humid day on Guadalcanal in June, 1943. The 148th Infantry Regiment, Young's outfit, was girding for its next objective—New Georgia Island with its insignificant but strategically vital Munda airstrip.

The company commander was busy that morning. He looked up sharply when Rodger Young, a thin, pale, and bespectacled staff sergeant, walked into his tent, saluted and said: "Sir, I would like to request permission to be reduced to the rank of private."

It was an odd request. "What is your reason for wanting to be busted, Sergeant?" the captain replied brusquely.

"Well, sir——" The little sergeant reddened, and continued haltingly, "Well, you see, my ears are going bad. I can't hear very well any more." He swallowed, and then finished in a rush. "And I don't want any of my men killed in New Georgia because of me."

The C.O.'s eyes narrowed suspiciously. Was this a new twist in the technique of getting invalided home? "What's the matter, Sergeant?" he barked. "Don't you want to fight?"

Young stiffened. "Sir," he said distinctly, "I don't want to leave the outfit. I want to go—but as a buck private, so I'm only responsible for myself. I don't want to get anyone hurt because of me." His voice was thin and firm. "If I thought I'd be left behind because of this, then I'd rather drop the whole thing."

He half sold the captain, and an hour later the company doctor confirmed Young's story. The sergeant's ears were in bad shape.

"Shall we send him to the field hospital?" the doctor asked.

"No!" Rodger Young answered emphatically.

The doctor shrugged and the captain made a gruff apology. He promised to get Sergeant Young reduced to the rank of private "without prejudice." And the incident was forgotten.

Three weeks later, the 148th Regiment (along with the rest of the Thirty-seventh Division, "Ohio's Own") invaded New Georgia. The jungle was an almost impenetrable wall of vines and tangled undergrowth. The insects were unbearable, the food miserable, the water supply inadequate. At night, the 148th dug foxholes in mud and limestone. And, of course, there was always the enemy.

They crept in like animals by night, attacked, and vanished at dawn. With the invasion still only a beachhead, a good many men of the 148th were dead.

One evening, the tropic sun took its sudden plummet into blackness just as fifteen soldiers staggered into the company lines. Among them they carried five bodies, wrapped in blood-stained shelter halves. The lieutenant in charge of the ragged platoon made his report to the captain.

That morning, he had taken twenty men on a recon-
naissance patrol a mile in front of the lines. He had led his
men along an old, seemingly deserted Japanese trail, over-
grown with vines and bushes. After a futile search for signs
of enemy activity, he turned back at four o'clock, intend-
ing to be in his own company area before dusk.

As they trudged along the gloomy trail, the Jap machine
gun opened up suddenly, and killed two men before the
platoon could flatten into cover. The gun was fiendishly
placed on high ground, commanding the entire area. There
was no way around it, and to rush it meant sudden death.

The lieutenant attempted a mass maneuver with his remaining eighteen men, and two more died.

The situation was critical. If they could not break out of
the trap before nightfall, the Japs would move in. With
the machine gun cutting off the only possible avenue of es-
cape, the enemy was in no hurry.

The men were pressed into the ground. There was only
one hope. D Company might hear the spasmodic fire and
attack the machine-gun nest from the rear. There was
nothing to do but wait—and pray.

As it happens, prayers wouldn't have helped just then.
Company D was too busy defending its own position to
worry about a twenty-man platoon. And a little later it
wouldn't have mattered.

Each of those sixteen doomed men had his own thoughts.
No one knows what Private Rodger Young, flattened in
the scrub, was thinking. He might have been thinking of
his family, or of Clyde, the little Ohio town where he

grew up. He might have been thinking that he was only twenty-five years old, which is pretty young to die. Or he might merely have been thinking that the omnipresent Jap machine gun was a nuisance—and dangerous to boot.

What went on behind Young's spectacles and between his rather deaf ears no one knows. What is known is that he began to inch forward, cradling his rifle in his arms, past the lieutenant and toward the machine-gun nest.

The lieutenant saw him slither by, and tried to grab his leg. But Young was in a hurry and evaded his superior's grasp. Furthermore, the Japs saw the rustle of grass and loosed a burst that singed the lieutenant's hand and tore his collar.

"Come back here!" the lieutenant screamed at Young. "It's suicide. Come back—that's an order!"

Young hesitated a moment, then twisted his head around and grinned at the lieutenant. "I'm sorry, sir," he said, "but you know I don't hear very well."

He turned then, and continued to snake his way toward the Jap emplacement. They saw him coming, of course. A stuttering burst cracked into Young's left arm and splintered the stock of his rifle.

Young let the useless weapon drop. Still, he pressed forward. His buddies fired blindly at the emplacement, trying to divert the spitting stream of death. It didn't work.

Another burst of fire sewed a scarlet seam of holes down Young's left leg, from thigh to ankle. But he kept going, and finally reached a shallow hole about five yards from the machine gun. It was deep enough to afford him rather tenuous safety as the Japs apparently couldn't depress the muzzle of their gun far enough to get a clean shot at him.

"For God's sake, Young," the lieutenant shouted, "stay where you are! We'll get you out somehow."

Maybe that time Private Young really didn't hear. He might have been dying at that moment. In any case, he wasn't in the mood for playing possum.

Painfully, he reached into his belt with his good right hand for a grenade. He pulled the pin with his teeth. Then, rearing up and back—up out of his position of relative safety—he lobbed the grenade toward the machine gun.

The gun answered with a blast that caught him full in the face.

Rodger Young died as the grenade left his hand. Still, well thrown, it lit in the center of the machine-gun crew —and killed every one of the five Japs manning the weapon.

Within seconds, the fifteen survivors were on their interrupted way back to Company D. Silently they carried their five dead. Rodger Young didn't need to worry any more about being responsible for the lives of his buddies.

Two weeks later, the sweltering little island was in American hands. The troops stopped hunting and killing and began collecting themselves—and some well-earned medals. Company D's captain composed a lengthy recommendation that Private Rodger Young be awarded the Medal of Honor. One sentence read:

"Disregarding the orders of his platoon leader to come back, Rodger Young moved forward into the face of enemy fire." The regimental commander changed that to "Not hearing the orders . . ." No one in *his* regiment disobeyed orders, he remarked acidly.

The regimental commander also wrote a letter to the War Department, requesting that Young be promoted back to staff sergeant, posthumously. The War Department, which subsequently approved the Medal of Honor, denied the petition on the grounds that, in this case, Army regulations did not provide for posthumous promotion.

It might have ended there. But the War Department, while denying the posthumous promotion, did ponder Rodger Young's heroism long and carefully. And when, months later, song writer Frank Loesser sought out the single most dramatic and gallant act committed by a doughboy, the Rodger Young story was shown to him. He had to read it only once.

A military citation is a strange place in which to find inspiration for a ballad. But from just such a dispassionate source sprang the moving ballad of Rodger Young. On the face of it, it is a song commemorating the gallantry of one soldier. But when you hear it sung, you know that there is more than one Rodger Young, just as there are many islands in the South Pacific that knew Rodger Young's kind of glory. Consider the words:

> *Oh, they've got no time for glory in the Infantry,*
> *They've got no use for phrases loudly sung,*
> *But in every soldier's heart in all the Infantry*
> *Shines the name, shines the name of Rodger Young.*

It is plain that the name, and the story, of Rodger Young will live. And as the years go by, the fact that he was small and rather spindly, the fact that he needed powerful glasses, the fact that he asked to be demoted because he was going deaf and did not want that disability to jeopardize the lives of his comrades—these will fade from memory.

His name and his story will long outlive such details, and will become inseparably merged.

For some day, long after the last trace of war has vanished from those quiet Pacific Islands, Rodger Young will take his place among the legendary heroes of American history. And there he will be quite at home.

MEMORIAL DAY

☆

by Joyce Kilmer

Sergeant Kilmer of the famous Fighting Sixty-ninth was killed
in action in the Second Battle of the Marne, World War 1

☆

"Dulce et decorum est"

The bugle echoes shrill and sweet,
But not of war it sings today.
The road is rhythmic with the feet
Of men-at-arms who come to pray.

The roses blossom white and red
On tombs where weary soldiers lie;
Flags wave above the honored dead
And martial music cleaves the sky.

Above their wreath-strewn graves we kneel,
They kept the faith and fought the fight.
Through flying lead and crimson steel
They plunged for Freedom and the Right.

May we, their grateful children, learn
Their strength, who lie beneath this sod;
They went through fire and death to earn
At last the accolade of God.

In shining rank on rank arrayed
They march, the legions of the Lord;
He is their Captain unafraid,
The Prince of Peace . . . Who brought a sword.

CONSECRATION
by Marine Corporal Vin Cassidy, 1944

My heart and soul
I consecrate,
My life to him
I dedicate.
I fight for him,
I fight that he
May be what I
Had hoped to be.

I fight and pray
That wars shall cease;
That his shall be
A world at peace;
His dreams, my dreams
And all his plans.
His name—my son,
And every man's.

☆

LORD, WHILE FOR ALL MANKIND WE PRAY

☆

by John Wreford (1800-81)

☆

Lord, while for all mankind we pray
Of every clime and coast,
O hear us for our native land,
The land we love the most.

O guard our shores from every foe;
With peace our borders bless;
With prosp'rous times our cities crown,
Our fields with plenteousness.

Unite us in the sacred love
Of knowledge, truth and Thee,
And let our hills and valleys shout
The songs of liberty.

Lord of the nations, thus to Thee
Our country we commend;
Be Thou our refuge and our trust,
Her everlasting friend.

☆

THANKSGIVING

☆

Republic Steel Corporation

☆

The Pilgrims of 1621 . . . *they had so little* . . . Yet they
found it in their hearts to give Thanks for what they had.

We Americans of 1951 . . . *we have so much* . . . We,
too, give Thanks for what *we* have.

We have Freedom . . .   God's richest gift
And today
The lingering hope
Of the oppressed
In other lands.

For that Freedom
We give Thanks.

We have Courage . . .   To defend the
Cause of Freedom
"With our lives
Our fortunes and
Our sacred honor."

For that Courage
We give Thanks.

We have Memories . . .   We do not forget
American bravery

And sacrifice at
Valley Forge
Tripoli
The Alamo
Gettysburg
San Juan Hill
The Argonne
Normandy Beaches
Iwo Jima
And Korea.

For those Memories
We give Thanks.

We have Faith . . .   In God
In Nations
In Man
And in ourselves.

For that Faith
We give Thanks.

We have Hope . . .   That all peoples
Of God's world
Will be united
In everlasting Peace.

For that Hope
We give Thanks.

We have the Bell . . .　　　The Liberty Bell
　　　　　　　　　　　　Whose inspiring
　　　　　　　　　　　　Chimes now echo
　　　　　　　　　　　　On foreign shores
　　　　　　　　　　　　And whose
　　　　　　　　　　　　Song of Freedom
　　　　　　　　　　　　Is drowning out
　　　　　　　　　　　　The bloody dirge
　　　　　　　　　　　　Of communism.

　　　　　　　　　　　　For that Bell
　　　　　　　　　　　　We give Thanks.

We have Unity . . .　　　Though we may
　　　　　　　　　　　　Disagree
　　　　　　　　　　　　Among ourselves,
　　　　　　　　　　　　At any real threat
　　　　　　　　　　　　To our Freedom
　　　　　　　　　　　　A *united* America
　　　　　　　　　　　　Rises in her might.

　　　　　　　　　　　　For that Unity
　　　　　　　　　　　　We give Thanks.

We have Wisdom . . .　　　To know that
　　　　　　　　　　　　There are many
　　　　　　　　　　　　Enemies *at home*
　　　　　　　　　　　　Who seek
　　　　　　　　　　　　Stealthily to
　　　　　　　　　　　　Take our Freedoms

From us,
From our children
And our children's
Children.

For that Wisdom
We give Thanks.

And so we pray: Give to us all
The strength
To *keep* Freedom
At home . . .
To spread Freedom
Abroad . . .
To pass Freedom
On to the
Next generation
And to unborn
Generations
In a world
At peace.

WHAT AMERICA MEANS TO ME

☆

by Dean Alfange

1959

☆

America is not just rich in material things, an industrial giant, a mighty military power. America is the country schoolhouse, the village church, the town meeting, the humble farmhouse, the rhythmic poetry of peaceful countryside.

America is the mirth and laughter of its children, the charity, the generosity, the compassion of its people. America is the triumph of merit and diligence over family and caste. America is the freedom of choice which God intended all men to have—the right to do, to speak, to worship, to dissent, to dream, to build, to fail, and to succeed.

America is the marriage of liberty with authority, of individual freedom with social organization. America is the best discovery yet of a full and honorable way of life.

We are rich in all the things that decent people yearn for. It is our task to live up to these values and to make them known to every nation, friend or foe. For on us has fallen the challenge to lead the free. And the truth about ourselves is more powerful than any man-made missile.

☆

THE MEANING OF DEMOCRACY

☆

by Henry Ward Beecher (1813-87)
American Congregational Minister
From "National Unity," spoken in Plymouth Church,
November 18, 1869

☆

Democracy does not mean a universal level. It does not mean compulsory equality. It means equitable opportunity. . . . . . All that can be rightfully demanded is, that all men shall have education, for their full development; opportunity, for the use of their powers; protection, from the grasp and greed of unjust passions in their fellow men. After that men must find their own level. The liberty of becoming all that God gave a man the power of being, is all a true philosophy can demand.

TO AMERICAN CITIZENS OF FOREIGN BIRTH

☆

by *Woodrow Wilson*

An address to newly naturalized citizens, Philadelphia, May 3, 1915

☆

It warms my heart that you should give me such a reception; but it is not of myself that I wish to think tonight, but of those who have just become citizens of the United States.

This is the only country in the world which experiences this constant and repeated rebirth. Other countries depend upon the multiplication of their own native people. This country is constantly drinking strength out of new sources by the voluntary association with it of great bodies of strong men and forward-looking women out of other lands. And so by the gift of the free will of independent people it is being constantly renewed from generation to generation by the same process by which it was originally created. It is as if humanity had determined to see to it that this great nation, founded for the benefit of humanity, should not lack for the allegiance of the people of the world.

You have just taken an oath of allegiance to the United States. Of allegiance to whom? Of allegiance to no one, unless it be to God—certainly not of allegiance to those who temporarily represent this great government. You have taken an oath of allegiance to a great deal, to a great body of principles, to a great hope of the human race. You have said, "We are going to America not only to earn a living, not only to seek the things which it was more difficult to obtain where we were born, but to help forward the great enterprises of the human spirit—to let men know that everywhere in the world there are men who will cross strange oceans and go where a speech is spoken which is alien to them if they can but satisfy their quest for what their spirits crave; knowing that whatever the speech, there is but one longing and utterance of the human heart, and that is for liberty and justice." And while you bring all countries with you, you come with a purpose of leaving all other countries behind you—bringing what is best of their spirit, but not looking over your shoulders and seeking to perpetuate what you intended to leave behind in them. I certainly would not be one even to suggest that a man cease to love the home of his birth and the nation of his origin—these things are very sacred and ought not to be put out of our hearts—but it is one thing to love the place where you were born and it is another thing to dedicate yourself to the place to which you go. You cannot dedicate yourself to America unless you become in every respect and with every purpose of your will thorough Americans. You cannot become thorough Americans if you think of yourselves in groups. America does not consist of groups. A man who thinks of himself as belonging to a particular national group in America has not yet become an American, and the man who goes among you to trade upon your nationality is no worthy son to live under the Stars and Stripes.

My urgent advice to you would be, not only always to think first of America, but always, also, to think first of humanity. You do not love humanity if you seek to divide humanity into jealous camps. Humanity can be welded together only by love, by sympathy, by justice, not by jealousy and hatred. I am sorry for the man who seeks to make personal capital out of the passions of his fellowmen. He has lost the touch and ideal of America. For America was created to unite mankind by those passions which lift and not by the passions which separate and debase. We came to America, either ourselves or in the persons of our ancestors, to better the ideals of men, to make them see finer things than they had seen before, to get rid of the things that divide and to make sure of the things that unite. It was but an historical accident no doubt that this great country was called the "United States"; yet I am very thankful that it has that word "United" in its title, and the man who seeks to divide man from man, group from group, interest from interest in this great Union is striking at its very heart.

It is a very interesting circumstance to me, in thinking of those of you who have just sworn allegiance to this great Government, that you were drawn across the ocean by some beckoning finger of hope, by some belief, by some vision of a new kind of justice, by some expectation of a better kind of life. No doubt you have been disappointed in some of us. Some of us are very disappointing. No doubt you have found that justice in the United States goes only with a pure heart and a right purpose, as it does everywhere else in the world. No doubt what you found here did not seem touched for you, after all, with the complete beauty of the ideal which you had conceived beforehand.

☆

But remember this: If we had grown at all poor in the ideal, you brought some of it with you. A man does not hope for the thing that he does not believe in, and if some of us have forgotten what America believed in, you, at any rate, imported in your own hearts a renewal of the belief. That is the reason that I, for one, make you welcome. If I have in any degree forgotten what America was intended for, I will thank God if you will remind me. I was born in America. You dreamed dreams of what America was to be, and I hope you brought the dreams with you. No man that does not see visions will ever realize any high hope or undertake any high enterprise. Just because you brought dreams with you, America is more likely to realize dreams such as you brought. You are enriching us if you came expecting us to be better than we are.

You have come to this great nation voluntarily seeking something that we have to give, and all that we have to give is this: We cannot exempt you from work. No man is exempt from work anywhere in the world. We cannot exempt you from the strife and the heartbreaking burden of the struggle of the day—that is common to mankind everywhere; we cannot exempt you from the loads that you must carry. We can only make them light by the spirit in which they are carried. That is the spirit of hope, it is the spirit of liberty, it is the spirit of justice.

298

IN GOD WE TRUST

. . . do we or don't we?

Does it mean anything . . . or doesn't it?

Would another phrase do just as well? Our nation's founders didn't think so!

The men who signed the Constitution . . . the men—and women—who braved the prairie and the mountain to pioneer our land . . . they didn't think so.

But what about us? Does this motto on the coin in our pocket guide us . . . inspire us . . . strengthen us? Or have we forgotten the power of the faith expressed in these words?

If our country's future is uncertain . . . if we are worried about tomorrow . . . then perhaps the time has come to put aside small things and turn once more to the faiths which made our nation great.

Our country's great leaders down through the years have shared a sure belief in God . . . in themselves . . . in their fellow men . . . and in freedom! In crisis and in peace they have placed their faith in God's wisdom . . . and in their own ability to work out their problems . . . and in the great justice of a free people.

Let us do the same today. For these faiths will renew our strength.

HAVE FAITH

In God
In Ourselves
In Our Fellow Men
In Freedom

Texas and Pacific Railway

☆

AMERICA, THE BEAUTIFUL

☆

by Katherine Lee Bates (1859-1929)

☆

O beautiful for spacious skies,
For amber waves of grain,
For purple mountain majesties
Above the fruited plain.
America! America!
God shed His grace on thee,
And crown thy good with brotherhood
From sea to shining sea.

O beautiful for pilgrim feet
Whose stern impassion'd stress
A thoroughfare of freedom beat
Across the wilderness.
America! America!
God mend thine ev'ry flaw,
Confirm thy soul in self-control,
Thy liberty in law.

O beautiful for heroes prov'd
In liberating strife,
Who more than self their country loved,
And mercy more than life.
America! America!
May God thy gold refine

Till all success be nobleness,
And ev'ry gain divine.

O beautiful for patriot dream
That sees beyond the years;
Thine alabaster cities gleam
Undimmed by human tears.
America! America!
God shed His grace on thee,
And crown thy good with brotherhood
From sea to shining sea.

☆

ONLY A RACCOON

☆

by *Lawrence E. Hunt*

☆

We joined the crowd around a cage containing two brown
bears and a pair of raccoons at the San Francisco zoo. Beside me was a little foreigner who, like everyone else, was
laughing at one of the bears which sat, arms spread wide,
begging for peanuts. When my daughter began throwing
candied popcorn to one of the 'coons, the bear walked
over and pushed the 'coon roughly aside. Instantly there
were shouts from the crowd: "Leave that 'coon alone!"
"Go pick on somebody your own size!"

The 'coon, seemingly encouraged, darted forward, sank
its teeth in the bear's forepaw and leaped nimbly back.
There was another roar from the crowd. "Good for you!"
"That's showing the big bum!"

I noticed that the little foreigner wasn't laughing with
the rest. He seemed to be almost crying. But he wasn't em-
barrassed by my stare. "Ach," he said, "that's why I love
America so. Over here they all cheer for the little fellow
—even if it's only an animal."

OUR COUNTRY

☆

by *Daniel Webster*

From an address at the laying of the cornerstone of
Bunker Hill Monument, June 17, 1825.

☆

Let our object be our country, our whole country, and
nothing but our country. And, by the blessing of God, may
that country itself become a vast and splendid monument,
not of oppression and terror, but of Wisdom, of Peace, and
of Liberty, upon which the world may gaze with admiration forever.

ARLINGTON—WHERE SLEEP THE BRAVE

☆

by *Donald Culross Peattie*

1952

☆

The most sacred ground in America is a few square feet of Virginia soil just across the Potomac from Washington. It is more hallowed than any battlefield; for here, upon what was once part of the estate of General Robert E. Lee, rests in honored glory a soldier greater than even he—"an American soldier known but to God."

To Arlington National Cemetery come every year more than two million pilgrims. Not to the Tomb of the Unknown Soldier alone do they come to pay homage, but to the multitude of his honored comrades in arms who sleep in the leafy acres around him.

By many a strange turn of fate did Arlington, once a forested wilderness, come to be the final sanctuary of our illustrious dead. It is part of 6,000 acres deeded by Governor Berkeley of Virginia in 1669 to a ship's captain, as return for bringing a fresh load of colonists. The captain promptly traded this land for six hogsheads of tobacco. And so it kept changing hands, more or less in speculation, until in 1778 it passed into the possession of John Parke Custis, son of Martha Washington by her first husband. He began to work it as a plantation, and in 1802 his son, George Washington Parke Custis, began to build Arlington House, which today you still see, shining out upon the forested heights of the Virginia shore.

Its lofty portico of white columns was fondly believed by its builder to reproduce the temple of Theseus at Athens, but it looks to our eyes just what it is, and ought to be—a typical old southern mansion, fit scene for the wedding, in 1831, of young Lieutenant Robert Edward Lee to the owner's daughter, Mary Ann Randolph Custis. In time she inherited mansion and plantation, and here she and her husband were living happily when the storm clouds of the Civil War gathered. From Arlington, one April day in 1861, Lee rode over the Potomac, at a call from the War Department, and there heard himself offered the command of the Union Armies. To answer either way was heartbreak. Detesting slavery, Lee had freed all his slaves; yet he could not draw his sword against his kin and neighbors. So he rode back, that warm spring night, to the house on the wooded height, filled with the heavy premonition that he was about to leave Arlington forever.

In two days he was on his way to Richmond to offer that stainless sword to the state of Virginia. A month later Mrs. Lee and the children followed him. Swiftly Union forces occupied Arlington, a position essential to the defense of the capital. Swiftly ancient trees came crashing down, as ground was cleared for powerful Fort Whipple (now Fort Myer) and Fort McPherson, whose earthworks are still seen. On the plowed fields of the farm, McClellan drilled his raw recruits. The lovely mansion echoed to the tramp of boots; looters carried off many of its treasures.

Powerless to protect her home, Mrs. Lee in Richmond was nonetheless receiving notices of taxes due on Arlington. They were only twelve dollars a year, and she sent them promptly by an emissary. But they were refused on the illegal grounds that she must appear with them in person. As she would not enter so obvious a trap, the estate was at last put up at auction, for delinquent taxes. In January, 1864, it was bought in by the United States Commissioners.

Vicksburg and Gettysburg had been fought and won, and the end of the conflict could be seen afar, but long was the road and bloody. The hospitals of Washington were crowded with wounded, both Union and Confederate, and from them many, too many, came forth as dead. Quartermaster General Meigs suggested to President Lincoln that Arlington be dedicated as a national cemetery, and in June Secretary of War Stanton so authorized. But already "Taps" had sounded here over turned earth beneath the great old trees. Officially or not, the first soldier had been buried here a month earlier. Soon the sad bugle blew again and again, over the Blue and the Gray alike. From the battlefields of northern Virginia alone were gathered the bones of 2,111 Union soldiers. They were placed in a single grave.

But even the bloodiest war spends its last red drops. When it was over, when General and Mrs. Lee too were gone, their eldest son sued the United States Government for recovery of his estate. George Washington Custis Lee's legal battle went on for years, till it reached the Supreme Court, which gave the Lees justice at last. Technically, Mr. Lee might have required the removal of all those buried on Arlington's slopes. But instead he agreed to relinquish his claims and sell the property for the sum—modest even in those days—of $150,000. In 1883 Congress appropriated the money and accepted the deed. And in 1925 Arlington House was restored to its old gracious beauty, with many authentic mementos of the Lees and copies of their original furniture, so that today it is thronged with delighted visitors.

The acres around the old home, some four hundred of them, offer a final resting place not only to our heroes killed in action but to any honorably discharged veteran, his wife and minor children and to Army and Navy nurses. Each is provided with a simple headstone. Any grander monuments are erected at the expense of friends or organizations, or by special act of Congress. But there are few "high-horse" statues here. Even General Pershing, by his wish, lies under a simple block. Rear Admiral Robert Peary, discoverer of the North Pole, is honored by a stone globe, put up by the National Geographic Society. Men of the Coast Guard are memorialized by a sea gull poised before a rocky pyramid.

In the great democracy of death, generals and admirals rest beside privates and seamen. Together they represent service in all the wars fought to keep our country free. There are graves, only a few but precious, of men who fought in the Revolution.

The nation recognizes that some of its greatest servants never wore uniform, and so Arlington includes civilians of the highest offices; thus President Taft and Secretary of Defense Forrestal lie here. Foreign soldiers who die while on duty in the United States may also be entombed in Arlington, which explains the imposing monument to Sir John Dill. So too there came here the great Polish statesman and pianist, Paderewski. He died in this country after his native land had fallen victim to the Russians.

No other cemetery has so little grief in it. The only shadows are of the ancient trees, elms and oaks, magnolias and dogwoods. Despite whatever carnage and agony brought many of these men to lie here, a shining peace prevails, visible and eloquent.

Dazzling white upon the brow of Arlington Heights gleams the memorial amphitheater, its Vermont marble sharp against the soft Virginia sky. On the marble benches of this open-air theater may be seated some four thousand persons, and another one thousand in the stately Doric colonnade that surrounds it. Here it is that crowds press in for the Easter sunrise service and observances on Memorial and Armistice days. And indeed many times a year do patriotic and civic groups meet here to pay honor to the nation's dead.

It was on Armistice Day in 1921 that the Unknown Soldier was brought to this spot. Never were such precautions taken to establish the *lack* of identity. From each of the four American battlefield cemeteries in France had been selected a body known by uniform and equipment to be American, while gunshot wounds proved death in battle, and absence of identification established anonymity. All four were placed in identical caskets and taken to Chalons-sur-Marne. Then, to the strains of a hymn from a military band, Sergeant Edward F. Younger (who now also rests at Arlington) walked slowly around the caskets, and at last solemnly laid upon one of them a wreath of red roses.

The United States cruiser *Olympia* bore the flag-draped

casket, past the French fleet thundering salute, across the sea to Washington. By caisson it was transferred to the rotunda of the Capitol, where Presidents have lain in state, and for two days a stream of visitors paid it honor. At 8:30 on the morning of Armistice Day, Washington heard the first salvos of the minute guns from Fort Myer, which continued, at sixty-second intervals, for the five hours of ceremony that followed.

At last the procession to Arlington, the speeches, the hymns, the anthems, the commitment to the catafalque, where the casket rests forever upon soil gathered from the American battlefields in France, the reverent laying of wreaths, the ultimate benediction, the slow bugle notes of "Taps," the three salvos, crashing and final, of the minute guns—at last they are over, and the crowd is dispersed.

Today there is only the snapping of the flag upon the pole, the rhythmic tramp of the sentry, up and down, all day, all night, in sun or storm, the never-ending vigil. Throughout the years this sentry has walked his post by a military clockwork of paces and turns that takes exactly one minute to execute. Every hour the guard is changed, the Tomb saluted again. All the sentries are volunteers.

Day after day come dignitaries, our own and foreign, to lay official tributes at the Tomb. On my last visit I watched such a ceremony, complete with ambassador, silk hats, and dress swords. The color guard was turned out for the occasion, performing its faultless and dramatic evolutions. A bit later another group arrived with a wreath—some Boy and Girl Scouts from a small town in Maryland. There were no silk hats, but again the color guard turned out in full, again sounded the sergeant's bark, the thump and clash of arms presented.

The boy and girl who had been chosen to carry the wreath together offered their tribute as humbly as a prayer. Both were awed, visibly. So was I. When the youngsters had filed away, when the last notes of "Taps" had floated away over the Tomb, when only the sentry remained at his endless pacing, eternity was so silent you could hear a white-throat sparrow singing his Sweet, sweet, sweet! "Sweet and fitting"—*dulce et decorum*—"is it to die for one's country."

THE UNKNOWN SOLDIER

☆

by Virginia Eaton

1939

☆

How peacefully he sleeps out there
In Arlington, among the fair
Hills of Virginia. Loving hands
Have brought him back from foreign lands
Across the sea that he may rest
Within the land that he loved best
And died to save! There is no name
Upon his tomb to tell of fame,
Or honor that he may have won
Upon the battlefields; his name
Passed with his passing soul, and still
A Nation honors him and will
Through all the years to come. We know
He is the emblem of that flow—
That living tide—the boys who gave
Their lives, their own fair land to save.
Your boy or mine? Ah, who can tell?
A husband, sweetheart? It were well
To call him Ours—both yours and mine—
And bow with reverence at his shrine.

HE IS THE STRANGER WHO IS MY BROTHER

☆

John Hancock Mutual Life Insurance Company

1950, 1951

☆

This is the story of a man I never knew, and yet I know all about him.

He is dead now, and he lies in a tomb of polished marble whose splendor would surprise him. And people come from everywhere to stand here with their heads bowed, their eyes serious, their hearts filled with mourning for this man they never knew.

Because he wore a uniform when he died, they call him the Unknown Soldier. I think he was a good soldier, though fighting was never his business. He was a man of peace, I'm sure, though he never told me.

He was born on a farm in the Dakotas . . . or was it a miner's cottage in Pennsylvania, a tenement in the Bronx, a ranch house in Texas, a duplex apartment on Park Avenue? I can't be sure, as I stand here with my hat in my hand, reverent at the grave of this man I never knew.

I don't know his name or his business; whether his grammar was good, his accent like mine; what books he read; what church he went to; which way he voted; how much money he had.

Was he a poet, bookkeeper, truck driver, surgeon, lumberjack, errand boy, student? Was he telling a joke, or cursing his sergeant, or writing to his family, when the missile came?

I don't know. For when they picked this man, from among all our nameless dead, he was lying quiet in a closed coffin, and known only to God.

But I do know that he is deserving of honor and respect. For, whoever he may be, I feel sure he must have believed, as I do, in the equality of men, the promise of men, the duty of men to live justly with each other and with themselves.

And that is why I stand here with my hat in my hand, reverent at the grave of the stranger who is my brother, my father, my son, my countryman, my friend.

☆

INAUGURAL

☆

by *Alva Romanes*

For the Inauguration of Herbert Hoover, 1929

☆

Eternal Guide, within whose hand
The wheeling suns were wrought from dust,
Whose everlasting love has planned
Our road from darkness up to trust!
By You alone we walk aright;
So here in solemn faith we pray,
To seek the Spirit's lasting light
Upon Your servant's path today.

From lowly circumstance we came,
And humble was our lot from birth,
Before the thunder of our name
Had shaped the councils of the earth;
But if our strength, within Your eyes,
Has led us from the Truth astray,
Eternal Father! make him wise
Who takes our leadership today.

We are not for ourselves alone;
But for a Purpose wide and far
That beckons out to worlds unknown
Beyond the sky's remotest star.
Today we share the bounds of time;
Yet, gleaming faintly, we can see

A Goal immortal and sublime
That reaches to infinity.

Beyond the year's dividing veil
We hasten to the Inner Shrine;
Forever on the upward trail
We sense our part in things divine;
So hear, Eternal God! our prayer,
And guide Your servant on his way,
And bless, within Your servant's care,
The leadership he takes today.

☆

THE PRESIDENT PRAYS

☆

by *Ruth Gibbs Zwall*
April, 1956

☆

He kneels tonight in prayer:
His mind is heavy with tomorrow's care—
A thousand thoughts, a plan, the fret and strain . . .
Time like a pendulum swings back again
Across the running years; a mystic glow
Brings, one by one, the figures in the snow
Kneeling at Valley Forge; their voices blend
With his in prayer, as some beloved friend,
And speak across a mighty nation's length,
"God, give us strength."

Beyond the darkened room
The towns and cities lie; their peace and doom
Stand in the circle of his uttered prayer:
He sees the foes of freedom lurking there,
The many wrongs to right. And as he prays
For guidance through the tangled, troubled maze,
The gleam of some dim campfire brings them back—
Those shadowed forms beside their wagon pack,
Whose voices rise with his to merge and meet,
"Lord, guide our feet!"

He kneels to pray tonight,
Conscious of God, the changelessness of right,

A need in self and country to be true,
Wide harvest fields that tell of praises due.
And as he speaks, the brave of Plymouth speak
From out the free frontier they came to seek,
Joining his prayer—the man, the youth, the maid,
The mother, bowing simply, unafraid,
"Our God, we give thee thanks for life and bread,
Aye, for thyself, by whom our souls are fed;
For liberty wherein today we stand.
Lord, bless our land."

☆

WASHINGTON'S PRAYER
FOR THE
UNITED STATES OF AMERICA

☆

From a letter to the Governors of the Thirteen States, June 8, 1783

☆

. . . . . I now make it my earnest prayer, that God would have you . . . . . in His Holy Protection, that He would incline the hearts of the citizens to cultivate a spirit of subordination and obedience to government, to entertain a brotherly affection and love for one another, for their fellow citizens of the United States at large, and particularly for their brethren who have served in the Field, and finally, that He would most graciously be pleased to dispose us all, to do justice, to love mercy, and to demean ourselves with that charity, humility, and pacific temper of mind, which were the characteristics of the Divine Author of our blessed religion, and without a humble imitation of whose example in these things, we can never hope to be a happy Nation.

☆

by John F. Kennedy

January 20, 1961

☆

Vice-President Johnson, Mr. Speaker, Mr. Chief Justice, President Eisenhower, Vice-President Nixon, President Truman, Reverend Clergy, fellow citizens:

We observe today not a victory of party but a celebration of freedom—symbolizing an end as well as a beginning—signifying renewal as well as change. For I have sworn before you and almighty God the same solemn oath our forebears prescribed nearly a century and three-quarters ago.

The world is very different now. For man holds in his mortal hands the power to abolish all forms of human poverty and all forms of human life. And yet the same revolutionary beliefs for which our forebears fought are still at issue around the globe—the belief that the rights of man come not from the generosity of the state but from the hand of God.

We dare not forget today that we are the heirs of that first revolution. Let the word go forth from this time and place, to friend and foe alike, that the torch has been passed to a new generation of Americans—born in this century, tempered by war, disciplined by a hard and bitter peace, proud of our ancient heritage—and unwilling to witness or permit the slow undoing of those human rights to which this nation has always been committed, and to which we are committed today at home and around the world.

Let every nation know, whether it wishes us well or ill, that we shall pay any price, bear any burden, meet any hardship, support any friend, oppose any foe to assure the survival and the success of liberty.

This much we pledge—and more.

To those old allies whose cultural and spiritual origins we share, we pledge the loyalty of faithful friends. United, there is little we cannot do in a host of new cooperative ventures. Divided, there is little we can do—for we dare not meet a powerful challenge at odds and split asunder.

To those new states whom we welcome to the ranks of the free, we pledge our word that one form of colonial control shall not have passed away merely to be replaced by a far more iron tyranny. We shall not always expect to find them supporting our view. But we shall always hope to find them strongly supporting their own freedom—and to remember that, in the past, those who foolishly sought power by riding the back of the tiger ended up inside.

To those people in the huts and villages of half the globe struggling to break the bonds of mass misery, we pledge our best efforts to help them help themselves, for whatever period is required—not because the Communists may be doing it, not because we seek their votes, but because it is right. If a free society cannot help the many who are poor, it can not save the few who are rich.

To our sister republics south of our border, we offer a special pledge—to convert our good words into good deeds —in a new alliance for progress—to assist free men and free governments in casting off the chains of poverty. But this peaceful revolution of hope cannot become the prey of hostile powers. Let all our neighbors know that we shall join with them to oppose aggression or subversion anywhere in the Americas. And let every other power know that this hemisphere intends to remain the master of its own house.

To that world assembly of sovereign states, the United Nations, our last best hope in an age where the instruments of war have far outpaced the instruments of peace, we renew our pledge of support—to prevent it from becoming merely a forum for invective—to strengthen its shield of the new and the weak—and to enlarge the area in which its writ may run.

Finally, to those nations who would make themselves our adversary, we offer not a pledge but a request: that both sides begin anew the quest for peace, before the dark powers of destruction unleashed by science engulf all humanity in planned or accidental self-destruction.

We dare not tempt them with weakness. For only when our arms are sufficient beyond doubt can we be certain beyond doubt that they will never be employed.

But neither can two great and powerful groups of nations take comfort from our present course—both sides overburdened by the cost of modern weapons, both rightly alarmed by the steady spread of the deadly atom, yet both racing to alter that uncertain balance of terror that stays the hand of mankind's final war.

So let us begin anew—remembering on both sides that civility is not a sign of weakness, and sincerity is always subject to proof. Let us never negotiate out of fear. But let us never fear to negotiate.

☆

Let both sides explore what problems unite us instead of belaboring those problems which divide us.

Let both sides, for the first time, formulate serious and precise proposals for the inspection and control of arms—and bring the absolute power to destroy other nations under the absolute control of all nations.

Let both sides seek to invoke the wonders of science instead of its terrors. Together let us explore the stars, conquer the deserts, eradicate disease, tap the ocean depths and encourage the arts and commerce.

Let both sides unite to heed in all corners of the earth the command of Isaiah—to "undo the heavy burdens . . . [and] let the oppressed go free."

And if a beachhead of cooperation may push back the jungles of suspicion, let both sides join in creating a new endeavor—not a new balance of power, but a new world of law, where the strong are just and the weak secure and the peace preserved.

All this will not be finished in the first hundred days. Nor will it be finished in the first thousand days, nor in the life of this Administration, nor even perhaps in our lifetime on this planet. But let us begin.

In your hands, my fellow citizens, more than mine, will rest the final success or failure of our course. Since this country was founded, each generation of Americans has been summoned to give testimony to its national loyalty. The graves of young Amercians who answered the call to service surround the globe.

Now the trumpet summons us again—not as a call to bear arms, though arms we need—not as a call to battle, though embattled we are—but a call to bear the burden of a long twilight struggle year in and year out, "rejoicing in hope, patient in tribulation"—a struggle against the common enemies of man: tyranny, poverty, disease, and war itself.

Can we forge against these enemies a grand and global alliance, north and south, east and west, that can assure a more fruitful life for all mankind? Will you join in that historic effort?

In the long history of the world, only a few generations have been granted the role of defending freedom in its hour of maximum danger. I do not shrink from this responsibility—I welcome it. I do not believe that any of us would exchange places with any other people or any other generation. The energy, the faith, the devotion which we bring to this endeavor will light our country and all who serve it—and the glow from that fire can truly light the world.

And so, my fellow Americans: ask not what your country can do for you—ask what you can do for your country.

My fellow citizens of the world: ask not what America will do for you, but what together we can do for the freedom of man.

Finally, whether you are citizens of America or citizens of the world, ask of us here the same high standards of strength and sacrifice which we ask of you. With a good conscience our only sure reward, with history the final judge of our deeds, let us go forth to lead the land we love, asking His blessing and His help, but knowing that here on earth God's work must truly be our own.